Management standards for developing information systems

Norman L. Enger

Management standards for developing information systems

amacom
A DIVISION OF AMERICAN MANAGEMENT ASSOCIATIONS

Library of Congress Cataloging in Publication Data

Enger, Norman L
Management standards for developing information systems.

Bibliography: p. 205
Includes index.
1. Management information systems. I. Title.
HF5548.2.E54 658.4'03 76-41827
ISBN 0-8144-5425-9

Third Printing

TO MY MOTHER AND FATHER, NORA AND NILS

Preface

This book is directed toward corporate management—policy, middle, and data processing management. It provides nontechnical policy and middle management with guidelines for controlling and evaluating corporate information systems that are being developed. The manager of data processing is provided with a management skills profile against which he can match his own job performance.

Too many corporations have permitted a priesthood of technical experts to control, with little corporate management direction, the data processing resources of organizations. Because of the rising costs of data processing and the importance of data processing to daily corporate operations, nontechnical management must take an active interest in the management and development of computer-based information systems.

The development of computer-based systems requires the direct involvement of *all* levels of management. Policy management and middle management, for example, must define the objectives of the systems and prepare the organization for systems installation. The data processing manager must, in turn, properly manage his available resources and build responsive information systems.

Unfortunately, the rapid technical change in the computer industry has resulted in a lag in man's ability to manage the design and implementation of computer-based information systems effectively. Too often the objectives of systems are ill-defined by user management and are therefore impossible to achieve. Too often computer analysts and programmers are unable to plan their work and then meet time and cost budget estimates. A move toward more professionalism in the design and development of information systems would be welcomed by both users and the majority of the dedicated analysts and programmers in the computer industry.

Only recently has emphasis in the data processing industry started to shift from computer equipment to people and systems. At most corporate data centers, nonhardware costs—people, software, support, and education—now exceed computer equipment costs. This cost shift means that management—both technical and nontechnical—must become increasingly concerned with the control of developmental projects and the work performance of computer personnel.

This book guides management through the six major stages—initiation, analysis, design, development, implementation, operation—of an information systems development effort and outlines sixteen key documents that should be produced during this cycle. Within that framework, the control of the time, manpower, and cost required to build information systems should be possible.

The introduction to each chapter orients nontechnical policy and middle management and the data processing manager to the contents of the chapter. Chapter 1 of the book discusses the role of management in the development of information systems. Chapter 2 contains an overview of information system design principles and the proposed control structure. In Chapters 3 to 8 each phase in an information system development is related to the documents produced during that phase. Chapter 9 briefly summarizes some of the major points in the book.

I wish to thank my friend Dr. Paul Howerton, the recognized information scientist, for consenting to read and criticize the manuscript of this book. He read the draft several times and provided me with invaluable advice, guidance, and encouragement.

Much of the material in this book is based upon work that I have done for various industrial and governmental clients. Let me thank these many clients for the opportunity to view the benefits and problems of data processing from their perspective.

Elba Hernandez and Donna Adams labored over my handwriting and typed the draft several times. I wish to thank them for their patience.

Norman L. Enger

Contents

1.

The challenge to management

This book sets up guidelines for managing the design and implementation of data systems. Documents and techniques that are described in it simplify the control of work quality and progress. Also described is a standard format for the documentation of development work that simplifies the maintenance of systems, reduces the effect of personnel turnover, and provides a basis for the evaluation of project managers and developmental personnel. Overall, the control structure simplifies the development of effective systems by increasing management control of the development process.

Since the installation of the first commercial computer systems in the early 1950s, the data processing industry has been subject to rapid technical evolution. The early vacuum-tube systems that operated with limited capability and reliability have been superseded by complex, giant computer installations that are linked to remote terminals and cost millions of dollars annually to maintain and operate. By 1985, the handful of computer installations of the early 1950s will have proliferated to over 300,000 installations.

From a computer hardware viewpoint, vacuum tubes were replaced by transistors and then transistors were replaced by large-scale integration (LSI). From a computer software viewpoint, the simple control or executive software of early computers has been replaced by the large, complex executive programs of current systems. User application programs became more sophisticated with the shift toward an increased use of terminals, communications lines, and data management software.

THE ROLE OF MANAGEMENT

Unfortunately, rapid technical change has resulted in a lag in our ability to manage the design, implementation, and operation of computerized data systems effectively. Management principles vital to the control of data processing have not evolved in pace with technology. An article in the data processing magazine *Infosystems* discusses the problem: [1]

> Most of the failures we've witnessed over the years have been directly caused by inept management. And some of the successes have been in spite of management. In particular, most programming and systems analysis managers are characterized by a lack of training in management.
>
> We have known for years that one of the best ways to gain a poor systems analyst is to promote a programmer. Yet, somehow we expect these rules to be suspended when we promote our best technicians to management positions. This is another illustration of Peter's Principle.

Only recently, however, has emphasis in the data processing industry started to shift from computer hardware to people, software, support, and education. At most computer installations, people- and software-related costs now exceed computer equipment costs. The cost

[1] Jerry L. Ogdin, "The Mongolian Hordes Versus Superprogrammer," *Infosystems*, December 1972, p. 20.

shift means that management must become increasingly concerned with the control of developmental projects and the work performance of computer personnel.

Circuits for computer logic and storage continue to increase in switching speed, and the result is a dramatic improvement in computer performance per dollar cost. Computers delivered in 1985 are expected to have a tenfold improvement in circuit performance per dollar cost over those delivered in 1975. As computer speeds improve, computer time will decline in importance relative to such other resources as system analyst and programmer time. If techniques can be devised to reduce the system analyst and programmer time required to develop data systems, the productivity of most data processing organizations can be markedly improved.

Management controls and standards are needed to minimize time and cost overruns during the design and implementation of computer applications. Unfortunately, the short history of data processing is replete with software projects that were discarded after disastrous implementations or overruns. Computer professionals readily acknowledge the guesswork involved in estimating the resources necessary to develop a computer application of any complexity. An anonymous Air Force decision maker, quoted in the magazine *Datamation,* states: [2]

> You software guys are too much like the Weavers in the story about the Emperor and his new clothes. When I go out to check on a software development, the answers I get sound like, "We're fantastically busy weaving this magic cloth. Just wait a while and it'll look terrific." But there's nothing I can see or touch, no numbers I can relate to, no way to pick up signals that things aren't really all that great. And there are too many people I know who have come out at the end wearing a bunch of expensive rags or nothing at all.

Some of the symptoms of inadequate management standards are:

[2] Barry W. Boehm, "Software and Its Impact: A Quantitative Assessment," *Datamation,* May 1973, p. 48.

- Application development projects never seem to finish on time or at the estimated cost.
- Continual user changes to specifications disrupt and delay projects.
- Systems that become operational don't seem to satisfy user requirements.
- Strong user resistance impedes the installation of data systems.
- Operational systems seem to be machine- rather than people-oriented.
- There is a continual underestimation of the complexity of designing and implementing data systems.
- Project documentation is shallow and doesn't adequately define user responsibilities.
- Projects frequently enter a crisis state when they slip well beyond the scheduled date for operation.
- System documentation is weak because of the data processing staff's crisis mode of operation.
- Feasibility studies that justify applications from a cost/benefit point of view are seldom made.

In his book on the management of software projects, *The Mythical Man-Month*, Frederick P. Brooks, Jr.[3] compares these projects to prehistoric animals caught in tar pits:

> Large-system programming has over the past decade been such a tar pit, and many great and powerful beasts have thrashed violently in it. Most have emerged with running systems—few have met goals, schedules, and budgets. Large and small, massive or wiry, team after team has become entangled in the tar. No one thing seems to cause the difficulty—any particular paw can be pulled away. But the accumulation of simultaneous and interacting factors brings slower and slower motion.

[3] Reading, Mass.: Addison-Wesley Publishing Co., 1975.

The task of management is to organize manpower, equipment, and time resources to accomplish goals. A manager gets things done by working with people and resources to accomplish specific objectives. Management of data processing involves the usual concerns of management relative to leadership communication, organization, and education. However, there are several considerations unique to the data processing industry:

1. The role of the manager of data processing is ill-defined. The data processing industry has failed to define and promote professional and academic qualifications for data processing management.

2. There are serious shortages of well-qualified analysts, programmers, and operators. Therefore, the hiring of personnel, staffing of projects, and retention of talented people is a major management problem. The 250,000 systems analyst population of today is expected to grow to 750,000 by 1985.

3. Because of its newness, the data processing function often does not fit neatly into existing corporate structures. Its organizational location has been a problem for many firms. The data processing manager has often been placed in a position within the organizational structure that limits his effectiveness.

4. The rapid expansion of data processing applications in corporations has led to a cutting across of functional line departments. Therefore, the cooperation of middle and operating managers in line departments is vital to the successful implementation of data systems, and the data processing manager and his staff must actively solicit it.

5. Data systems often replace existing manual systems. A new computer system can rapidly create employee fears of layoffs or job reassignments. Therefore, the data processing manager and his staff must seek to calm unnecessary fears and overcome resistance to change.

6. The increasing complexity of data systems has made the education of users and data processing personnel more complicated, but the effective use of data processing requires substantial education and training of both groups.

7. The security, privacy, and confidentiality problem looms larger and larger. Data banks or files will be increasingly affected by federal, state, and local legislation. Management has become increasingly concerned with fraud, embezzlement, willful destruction, and natural hazards that can disrupt data processing.

8. Many currently operational data systems were poorly designed and inadequately documented. The operation and maintenance of these systems often requires an inordinate quantity of available manpower resources.

Effective data processing management requires selling skills as well as technical competence. The confidence of users must be gained while sometimes awesome technical resources are managed. The manager must be knowledgeable about a wide variety of equipment, software products, and applications.

The data processing manager must insure that he has obtained the maximum utilization of his resources while maintaining a high benefit return–to–cost ratio. In other words, he must adequately plan, organize, control, and communicate to implement responsive data systems. Good management can reduce the number of or eliminate ill-conceived, ill-designed data systems. The data processing manager must above all else be a manager, and too often his management training has not been recognized as necessary. He should have the following skills:

He must be able to sell the benefits to be derived from data processing, allay user fears, and win user cooperation.

He must have sufficient technical skill to manage technical data processing resources.

He must be able to manage people, evaluate alternative courses of action, and find workable solutions to problems.

He must be able to control resources and satisfy time schedules and budgetary limitations.

He must be able to advise top management on issues involving data systems. He must be able to communicate with top management effectively.

He must have the imagination and foresight to prepare three- and five-year data processing growth plans for his organization.

He must, by example, fair treatment, and ability to communicate, gain the loyalty and confidence of those working for him.

The desirable attributes of a data processing manager fall in these skill categories: leadership, communication, organization, technology, education, and economics.

LEADERSHIP

Leadership is required to develop professionalism in systems analysis and design, educate personnel in the development of efficient systems, and enforce systems design performance standards. The success of a standards program requires *direction* and motivation from management. Management is the force that motivates a staff of individuals to work toward common goals. It establishes the yardstick by which the success of a data system project will be measured. The leadership qualities of a good manager are usually a combination of basic personality, training, and experience.

Management *planning* provides a decision-making framework in which to control the development of data systems. Control involves choosing among alternative courses of action. The management planning function sets organizational objectives and the policies, procedures, and resources necessary to achieve the objectives. Management *control* seeks to assure that subsystems conform to plans. The manager guides and corrects activities to insure their conformity to corporate plans.

Many computer installations have multivolume handsomely bound sets of standards manuals that decorate the rooms rather than guide data systems development. Without the active support and interest of management, rules, standards, and policies become academic.

The implementation of a computerized polling project in the District of Columbia is an example of a mismanaged, poorly organized computer project that became a nightmare. A valid computer application—automated vote counting—was lost through poorly managed implementation. There simply was no management leadership. This description is from an article entitled "Washington Slept Here."

> A chain of errors, weighted by gross misunderstanding, dragged the election into a quagmire of accusations. Claims and counterclaims echoed in the halls of the District Building, the five-tiered wedding cake that houses city offices, which served as the foster home of Washington's short-lived dream machines. The vote tabulating system failed on that Election Day, and with it went Washington's rocky marriage of politics and technology.
>
> People made mistakes, machines were cranky, and organizations lost control. Pandemonium reigned. Seasoned professionals cracked under a barrage of unfamiliar pressures. Computer pros, hardened to the perversity of machines, were unable to cope with screaming reporters and their broadcast deadlines. Election officials, familiar with the demands of the press, were boggled by the unexpected rebellion of machinery that had worked just days before. Everybody and nobody seemed to be in charge.
>
> The causes of the confusion, like the ballots, may never be satisfactorily sorted out. So far, numerous meetings, several reports, and a host of allegations have established a few points of agreement and disclosed many unresolved conflicts. Lawsuits have been filed over the conduct of the election, and additional litigation has been mentioned by parties involved in the vote counting operation. The central issue, whether computers may be used successfully to speed election returns, was abandoned in the melee.[4]

[4] Reprinted from *Computer Decisions,* November 1974, page 28, copyright 1974, Hayden Publishing Company.

COMMUNICATION

Communication involves the transfer of information between individuals. The manager of data processing must communicate with policy, middle, and operating management and the internal data processing staff. He must have this widespread communication or the information systems that he is developing will fail.

The ability to communicate with policy management requires skill in presenting data processing issues in language and format that policy management can understand. A data processing manager cannot expect this level of management to understand the details of software and hardware configurations. He must keep policy management informed as to the potentials and limitations of data systems—especially the limitations. He must win the support and confidence of policy management.

Top management must be persuaded to support the data processing function as computer applications proliferate within the organizational structure and become vital to corporate competitiveness and survival. Information systems cannot succeed without the direct involvement of corporate management. In general, policy management does not feel comfortable with the powerful but troublesome resource known as data processing—the technology has appeared too suddenly and grown too rapidly.

Middle and operating management are the primary users of data processing in most corporations, and their support and understanding will usually determine the success or failure of data processing. Because of lack of communication between data processing personnel and middle management users, applications that should be relatively simple to automate often become confused and delayed in implementation. The manager of data processing must therefore make every effort to win the support of middle and operating management. Conflict between the data processing manager and middle and operating management has too often limited the effective utilization of data processing.

The data processing manager must also have good communication with the user environment, because data systems should be defined and developed in close dialogue with users. There should be good feedback from the environment to the manager on the effectiveness of existing data systems and the emergence of new requirements. If the manager works in isolation from the environment, there is little likelihood that the systems he is developing can be successfully installed. Also, most major data systems significantly affect the environment. New systems arouse fears of change in job functions. Therefore, the data processing manager must stress good communication with users to calm fears, win confidence, and smooth the transition to new data systems.

The manager's ability to communicate with his internal data processing staff will affect the motivations and loyalties of that staff. The employees in data processing—the programmers, analysts, and operators—are fully as important to efficient data processing as computer hardware and software. Unfortunately, that fact has been obscured by the glamour and ballyhoo surrounding each newly developed piece of computer hardware or software. The manager must win the loyalty and respect of those working for him through firm and fair treatment, knowledge of people, and ability to communicate with them.

ORGANIZATION

Corporations achieve specific goals by organizing people and resources to accomplish the goals. The manager defines the resources required for specific tasks, assembles them, assigns specific responsibilities, and monitors the accomplishment of the tasks.

The effectiveness of the data processing manager in performing those functions relates directly to the manager's own organizational placement in the corporate structure. If his placement makes him ineffectual, then data processing services in the organization will be unsatisfactory. In many major corporations, the data processing manager has or will eventually rise to a position involving corporate policy planning. That rise relates directly to the increased importance of data systems. More and more functions are being automated, and the evolutionary growth of information systems will be matched by a rise in importance of the data processing manager.

The involvement of all levels of management in the data processing function vastly increases the probability of function success. In many organizations, data processing has moved from placement within a line department such as finance to a department of administrative services or information systems. The shift reflects the role of data processing as a service to all organizational entities in a corporation and not just one line department.

One major issue in corporations that has implications crucial to the success of data processing is the division of responsibility between the user and the data processing staff. Most major corporations have established a corporate data processing staff to provide services to many line departments.

One approach is to centralize computer processing but decentralize data systems development and input preparation responsibilities. The user staff defines and develops data systems and is responsible for systems analysis, systems design, and programming. This decentralization of system development responsibility insures that users have their applications defined and programmed by personnel who are familiar with their internal operations and requirements.

Users have access to a corporate computer facility through a terminal or small satellite computer and retain input control, scheduling, quality, and distribution functions. A central data processing group controls system software development, training, and internal consulting. The user organization is responsible for decisions concerning their internal data processing organization, staffing, and control procedures.

Users either put data directly into a central computer system by means of remote terminals or send input data to the central facility. Input documents need not leave the user facility, and confidential reports can be printed there. Reports prepared at the center are routed to a user terminal or delivered by messenger service to the appropriate user.

In an alternative division of responsibilities (see Figure 1-1) the central data processing staff assumes all user systems and programming work and possibly the responsibility for all input data preparation. Centralization at this level—hardware, software, and applications development—can lead to significant problems. Users may believe that their unique application requirements are not understood in sufficient depth by the systems staff; and if user input preparation work has been assumed by the central staff, any unfamiliarity of that staff with user input forms and data can lead to quality control problems.

The data processing department itself can have several different structures. It can have a functional organization based on task specialization with separate managers for the programming and systems analysis activities, or it can have a project organization based on project leaders who supervise both the systems analysis and programming functions on major data systems. An alternative is for it to have a matrix organization based on a combination of the functional and project types. That structure would bc characteristic of a data processing organization with many short developmental efforts mixed with several long-term projects.

Finally, how the data processing manager organizes specific projects will determine the success or failure of the projects. The job definition and reporting systems established will have a significant effect, and the motivation the manager is able to instill in the project team members will determine speed and efficiency. Organization also means getting the user involved in systems definition and design, because the user has an understanding of the function that the computer is to support.

TECHNOLOGY

The rapidly changing computer technology has an important effect on the success or failure of the data processing manager. In ad-

Figure 1-1. Centralized information system development.

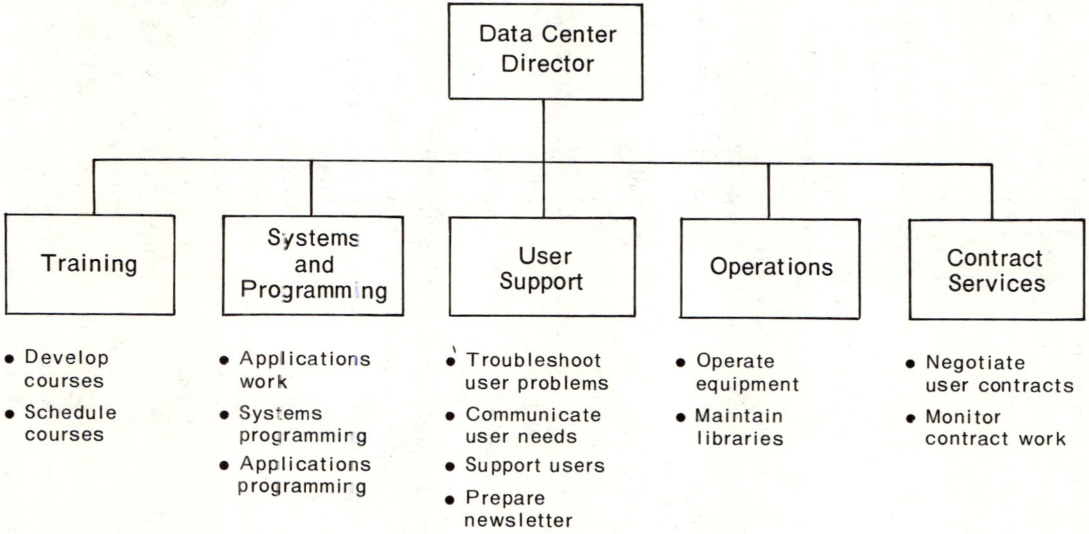

dition to being a good communicator and organizer, the manager must be conversant with computer systems, storage devices, communications, data management systems, and operating systems. His knowledge of behavioral science and human factors must be tied to his knowledge of computer technology.

In early 1974, Arthur D. Little, a management consulting firm, prepared a forecast of data processing technology through 1985 for the U.S. Air Force (*Support of Air Force Data Processing Requirements Through the 1980's*, AD-783-768, available from the National Technical Information Service, Springfield, Virginia). The report predicts that, by the 1980s, computers at today's performance level will cost one-tenth the present price and computers at today's medium-high price range will have speeds approaching 100 million instructions per second (MIPS).

Computer systems will consist of combinations of processors dedicated to such specialized functions as input/output control, file management, memory management, and interrupt processing. These complexes of component processors will automatically share microcoded instructions under control of the operating system in a manner largely invisible to the user. Microcoding will be utilized for such functions as scheduling, resource allocation, dynamic allocation of processor functions, automatic management of memory, and performance measurement. Networks of linked computers will be oriented around a single data base and central system supervisory software.

Data communications will be improved by the installation of more front-end communications computers and a drastic drop in the cost of communications computers and controllers. Data traffic volume through 1985 will continue to grow at a 35 percent annual rate, and there will be increased utilization of packet-switching technology to obtain rapid response times, high reliability, low error rates, dynamic allocation of transmission capacity, charges proportional to traffic volume, and improved transmission facilities. In computer peripheral technology, disk and tape densities up to forty times present capacities may become available and high-speed thermal printers will increase the output printing capacity of computer systems.

Software developments will lead to job control languages (JCL) becoming simpler and the COBOL and FORTRAN languages having more data base capability and more structured programming characteristics. More program development aids, such as language compilers oriented toward structured programming modules and software to generate test data automatically, will appear. Data management software will have features permitting improved record access and use statistics and improved data access control and security features.

The data processing manager must have enough familiarity with computer hardware and software technology to enable him to manage the company's computer resources intelligently. If he lets his knowledge and orientation fossilize, he will be unable to evaluate and utilize valuable technical advances properly.

EDUCATION

The data processing manager must not only continue his own education but also promote a corporate education program. Many executives rose to power before the widespread installation of computers. They often do not understand and are not comfortable with computer systems. An education program is therefore necessary. The objectives of the program for nontechnical management should be to develop an understanding of information systems, close the communication gap between nontechnical management and data processing, and familiarize the nontechnical manager with the capability of the computer to improve corporate productivity.

Friction between data processing and the line managers who use the data processing services retards the effective utilization of data processing. Line managers often do not understand the potentials, limitations, or requirements of data systems and are therefore unable to express their needs in terms that can be understood by the data services staff. The language failure leads to misunderstandings and recriminations.

It is necessary to educate all three levels of management—policy, middle, and operating—in the computer capabilities that are significant at each level. Users must be more involved in the definition and evaluation of computer applications, in the direction of feasibility studies, and in decisions on the modification or total redesign of existing systems. A productive dialogue must be established between the data processing staff and user personnel. The selection of new computer applications is too often left to computer technicians who have technical expertise but should not, by themselves, be directing corporate computer policy.

Because effective data system definition and evaluation depend on the education, support, and commitment of *all* levels of management, both data processing personnel and users must keep lines of communication open. There should be an introductory course for all user personnel in basic computer concepts with emphasis on application definition and design. The goal of the training should be to convey enough basic computer theory and language to users to simplify their dialogue with the corporate data processing program, but they cannot do so without a threshold of data processing knowledge.

The communications problem is solved by educating management in basic data processing principles while educating data processing people in company applications and operations. The data processing staff must also desire good communications and, to have them, must learn the business of the company for which they work. They must show less machine loyalty and more company loyalty. A systems analyst's inability to communicate with data processing users will prevent him from designing workable information systems.

The internal data processing staff also needs data processing education to keep abreast of the rapid technical change affecting supervisory software, data management systems, and communications systems. Education not only keeps the staff current with technology but also boosts morale. The job levels and job descriptions in the data processing department should relate directly to the education program.

Technically complex subjects with which the staff must become conversant include multiprogramming and multiprocessing, distributed computing, time sharing, and data management software. Programs written for terminal-oriented systems often must operate within severe response time and memory constraints. The terminals themselves may have varying operating characteristics, control codes, and transmission rates. The files on these terminal-oriented systems typically have billions of bytes of on-line information with complex access and retrieval structures.

The competence of the data processing staff to develop complex systems and programs relates directly to the relevance and quality of the training received. Management science techniques, including the use of simulation, linear programming, and general-purpose statistical techniques, will be more widely used, and staff members must be trained to work with operations research people on projects in which such techniques are used.

ECONOMICS

The data processing manager must have financial information to control the computer resource properly. He should be able to answer such questions as these:

How much money is being spent for a specific computer capability?
Is the money being spent effectively?
Does the payoff from the specific computer capability justify the cost?

The economics of data systems involves making sure that proposed computer applications are cost-justified. That requires a clear definition for each application of the user resources that are needed to develop and operate the information systems and the potential benefits.

The feasibility study for each major proposed data system should investigate alternative designs and justify the development of the system. A lack of understanding of computer capabilities or an inability to judge the value or cost of an application accurately leads to the automation of the wrong business aspects.

Cost control requires that the data processing manager operate within budgetary constraints. Managing the resources expended on developmental projects to insure that they do not encounter time and cost overruns is a major element of cost control. Each data system must be defined clearly enough to isolate the costs to develop and operate the system. Costs will accumulate against the system, and there should be a method of relating data system costs to progress and benefits.

The two basic methods of budgeting for data services are overhead accounting and cost center accounting. By the overhead accounting method, a fixed amount of money is allocated annually to the data processing division to cover computer costs and related service. That has several serious limitations:

- It is extremely difficult to relate cost to specific user projects.
- Users will tend to demand data processing service without regard to cost because they cannot relate their requests to costs.
- Users will usually have little incentive to insure that computer operations are efficient and effective.

With the overhead accounting method, it is usually not possible to analyze an operational data processing capability and answer such questions as how much it costs to develop the data system or operate it annually.

In the cost center approach, users are charged for their actual utilization of data processing resources. Some advantages of cost center operation are these:

- Users must allocate financial resources among various projects and thereby establish priorities.

- Management can tie costs directly to specific projects.
- The payoff from a project can be compared directly with the development cost.
- Users are made aware of the cost of their demands for data processing services.
- Users have more incentive for insuring that their computer center is cost-effective.

A computer service charging scheme implies a money management and distribution system. Other forms of "computer credit" systems have been devised, but the dollar system is favored because it is more comprehensible to managers who may or may not understand computer systems terminology. The operating capital outlay and all other budgets administered by managers are expressed in dollar terms.

Under a cost center structure, a published charging formula must be employed by data processing, and the charge rates must be designed to recover the cost of computer personnel, hardware, and software resources. Comprehensive systems management statistics should be collected by the computer center to track user demand for hardware, software, and other resources.

The machine accounting system is very important to cost center operations. It records the processing time, peripheral device time, and storage charges to be applied to the operation of the system. Those charges are billed to the user. The following categories of charges are generally utilized: central processor, unit record, setup time, storage, priority, personnel, terminal, and software.

For the typical computer system, charges are generally accumulated for central processor time and data input/output time. Unit charges are generally established for cards read, cards punched, and lines printed. Setup charges are usually imposed for operator handling of demountable tape and disk units and special forms and print chains. Storage charges are usually established for tape and disk file data storage to recover library maintenance costs. For remote terminals, a line-connect time charge is established to offset communications costs.

In a cost center operation systems analysis and programming personnel charges can be based on fixed hourly rates and operating personnel charges can be included in equipment utilization charges. The established rates would also include such data center overhead costs as administrative salaries and user services that are not billed directly to the user. Such services include user newsletter preparation and data center personnel time contributed to user committees and task forces.

A priority scheme featuring differential charges can be employed in a cost center operation to achieve load balancing and indirectly return scheduling decisions to the user organizations. For many users, turnaround time will be the most important resource they can purchase. Cost differentials can be associated with prime and nonprime shifts or with the priority levels that the user can assign to a job. The priority level assigned to a job will determine the amount of time the job must wait in a job queue for servicing at the computer center.

SUMMARY

The rapid technological evolution of computer systems has resulted in a lag in our ability to manage the design and implementation of information systems effectively. At most computer installations, people and software-related costs now exceed computer equipment costs. Management—both nontechnical and technical—must become increasingly concerned with the control of developmental projects and the work performance of data processing personnel. The following are some of the symptoms of inadequate management control of data processing:

Developmental projects never finish on time.
Operational systems don't satisfy user requirements.
Data systems are machine- and not people-oriented.
Middle management is hostile to data processing.
Data system documentation to justify data systems is poor.
Feasibility studies are seldom made.

The data processing manager should possess both selling skills and technical competence. He must manage technical resources and simultaneously win user confidence and support. He should possess skills in the following categories: leadership, communication, organization, technology, education, and economics.

Leadership involves management planning to organize the development of data systems and control to insure that subsystems conform to plans. The manager must communicate with policy, middle, and operating management and the internal data processing staff. He must obtain the involvement and commitment of those levels of management and win the loyalty and respect of his own data processing staff.

Policy management's placement of the data processing function in the corporate organization can determine success or failure of the function. Another consideration related to organization is the division of responsibilities for systems design, programming, data conversion, work scheduling, and similar functions between the user and data processing organizations. Finally, the internal organization of the data processing department along functional, project, or matrix lines will directly affect the efficiency of corporate data processing.

The data processing manager's knowledge of management science and human factors must be tied to a knowledge of computer technology. The manager must be conversant enough with hardware, software, and communications technology to be able to evaluate the quality of work being produced by the data processing staff and utilize technical advances. He should promote in his company a program to educate the policy, middle, and operating levels of management in the capabilities and limitations of data systems. The education program should seek to close the disruptive communications gap between user management and data processing. In turn, the data processing staff must become increasingly familiar with company applications and operations to communicate with and support users properly.

The data processing manager must also develop an economic or financial framework for the data processing resource. The framework should require feasibility studies for major data systems and a workable project control system to prevent time and cost overruns. The two basic methods of budgeting for data services are overhead accounting and cost center accounting. In overhead accounting a fixed sum of money is allocated annually to support the data processing function. In the cost center approach, user charges are based on utilization of data processing resources.

The successful implementation of information systems requires the following:

- Policy, middle, and operating management's commitment to and active involvement in data processing.
- User knowledge of and concurrence in the objectives of data systems.
- A data processing manager with both leadership and technical skills who can win the support and confidence of users.
- Systems analysts who can communicate with middle management and who understand the corporation's applications and operations.
- User recognition and acceptance of responsibilities associated with the development of new data systems.

2.

System development standards

Early data systems were developed as single applications, and little consideration was given to interapplication communication and data base structures. The systems were primarily clerical in nature and had such functions as payroll, inventory, and accounts receivable. By the third generation, in the late 1960s, computer systems had become more complex and more vital to corporate operations. In the future, corporate success will increasingly depend on the effectiveness with which the corporation can apply automation to all areas of business activity. Computers will be increasingly utilized to interpret and reduce external data for business decision making by corporation management. Figure 2-1 illustrates potential uses for corporate data systems.

SYSTEM DESIGN PRINCIPLES

A company utilizes money to obtain the manpower and material resources it needs to produce a commodity or service that is

Figure 2-1. Industrial systems.

I. SALES
- Sales forecast
- Sales analysis
  - By customer
  - By salesman
  - By region

II. ORDER EDITING
- Verify customer data
- Verify calculations

III. MATERIAL EXPLOSION
- Bill of material
- Master records

IV. INVENTORY
- Economic order quantities
- Safety stock/reorder point
- Raw materials/finished goods

V. PRODUCTION SCHEDULING
- Shop schedule
- Man scheduling

VI. ROUTING
- Operation sequence
- Operation instructions

VII. PARTS AND RAW MATERIAL STOCK
- Control issues
- Report issues to inventory

VIII. MACHINE LOAD
- Load by due date
- Over and under load data

IX. MANUFACTURING PROCESS
- Move tickets
- Job tickets

X. QUALITY CONTROL
- Optimum sample
- Reject control

XI. FINISHED STOCK
- Finished parts control
- Inventory notification

XII. INDUSTRIAL ENGINEERING
- Standard setup and operation
- Scientific subroutines
- Statistical subroutines

XIII. SHIPPING
- Packaging
- Ship products to customer

XIV. BILLING
- Produce customer invoice
- Freight analysis

XV. ACCOUNTS RECEIVABLE
- Update customer accounts
- Credit analysis

XVI. RECEIVING
- Receive vendor shipments
- Receive returned merchandise

XVII. QUALITY CONTROL
- Sample vendor shipments
- Report receipts to inventory

XVIII. ACCOUNTS PAYABLE
- Issue checks to vendors
- Forecast cash requirements

XIX. PAYROLL/PERSONNEL
- Write checks/labor distribution
- Personnel records

XX. GENERAL LEDGER
- Generate financial reports

marketed by a sales organization. The sale of the commodity or service produces additional capital that refuels the business/industrial cycle. The business/industrial functions shown in Figure 2-1 require these major systems:

1. *Sales system* to sell to customers the commodities or services produced by the company.
2. *Materials system* to stock and supply the raw materials and parts required for product production.
3. *Production system* to plan and schedule the manufacture of company products.
4. *Personnel system* to recruit and motivate managers, salesmen, engineers, machine operators, and other manpower.
5. *Financial system* to manage and control the accounts receivable, cash flow, accounts payable, general ledger, and other financial operations of the company.

Business organizations will increasingly depend on data systems to reduce volumes of internal and external data to manageable size. Computers will become more and more enmeshed in the methods and procedures employed by management to run the corporations. Data systems will evolve into the nerve structures of business and industrial firms and become vital to competitive survival. Figure 2-2 illustrates the data flow in a corporate information system.

Corporations have for several years been moving toward corporate information systems with a data base. Robert N. Anthony, in his book *Planning and Control Systems: A Framework for Analysis,* defines strategic planning, management control, and operational control as the three functions of management. These information systems support the planning control and operational functions of the corporation by providing information in the proper time frame to assist the management decision-making process.

The strategic planning role of management involves the selection of corporate objectives and the policies and resources required to attain those objectives. That is the executive decision-making realm, and it is

Figure 2-2. Corporate information system.

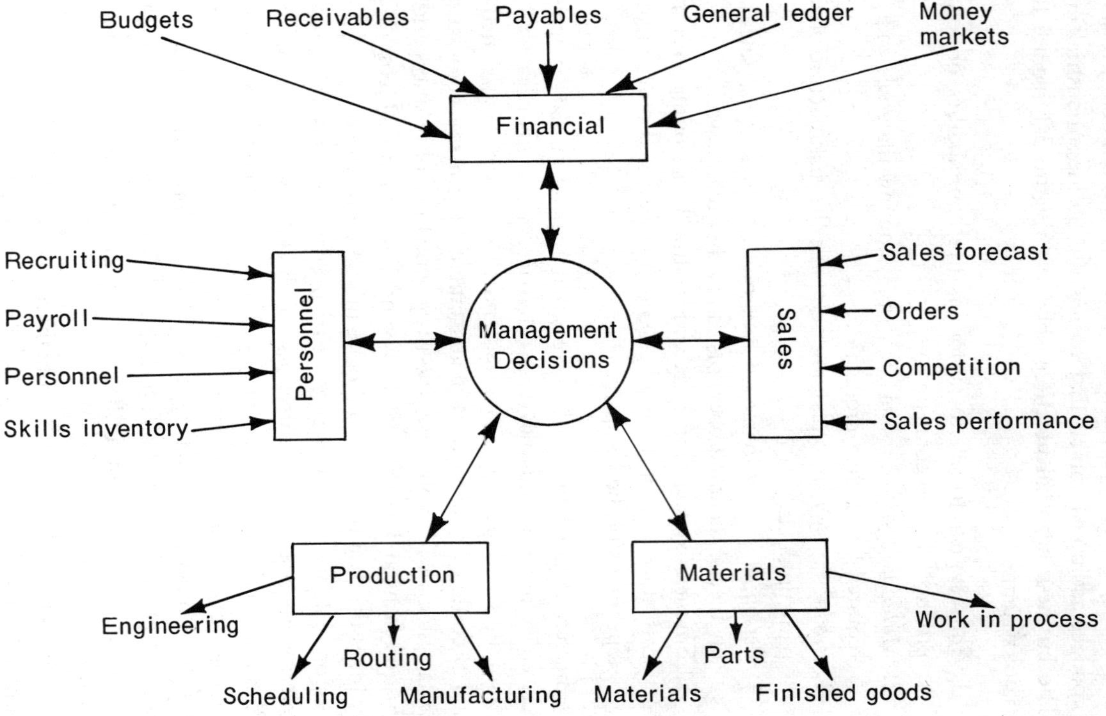

often difficult for the successful executive to explain the thought process he followed to arrive at a particular decision. The manager's intuition and creativity play a major role in strategic planning, and so the extent to which data systems can support management strategic planning is somewhat limited. Managers can, however, be aided by computers in this intuitive area by using them for simulation and modeling. Increased knowledge of and experience in the combined use of computer systems and management science techniques should supply strategic management with more precise methods for evaluating alternative courses of action.

The management control role requires the effective deployment and utilization of resources to attain objectives. Control is normally identified with line and middle management. Data systems can support this management function by supplying managers with faster and more accurate information applicable to such decisions as the assignment of people to jobs and the evaluation of job performance.

The operational control function of management seeks to insure that specific tasks are accomplished efficiently and effectively. The integration and, especially, the standardization of systems, the development of uniform rules and procedures, and the increase in the quality of information produced by data systems will have a profound effect upon this level of management decision making. Many of the routine decision-making functions of lower and middle management have been and will be greatly assisted by automated data systems.

Information systems can operate in either the batch processing or the on-line mode. Batch processing systems are dependent on the availability of input data and are scheduled for processing in a sequential or serial form. That means that a batch processing system is scheduled to run in a time-related manner based on the daily, monthly, and annual reporting requirements of the user. In contrast, on-line information systems can provide management with information on demand by means of terminals.

Real-time systems are on-line systems that receive transaction data, process the data, and produce output rapidly enough to influence the outcome of transactions. Airline reservations and on-line banking systems are examples of real-time systems. The airline reservation system permits the agent booking a reservation for a customer to utilize a display terminal to check space availability on flights and then book or wait-list a seat for the customer on a specific flight. The on-line banking system allows a bank teller to verify, by means of a terminal, the status of a customer account during a withdrawal transaction. Many business and industrial data systems that react rapidly to data inputs—the reaction time is known as response time—are real-time systems.

In real-time systems, the transactions used to update the master file are usually fairly short records. The systems have a high volume of a limited number of short, fixed input requests or transactions that are processed and answered by a few short responses quickly enough to satisfy the needs of management. Many data records may be brought to bear on the master file throughout the processing cycle, but individual data records are kept to minimum size to optimize the ability of the real-time system to accept, process, and react to the external environment. Responses in a real-time system are normally kept to an abbreviated form even when a fairly extensive equation may be part of a response.

Real-time commercial systems are normally supported by batch processing operations; the real-time (foreground) processing is predominant over the batch processing (background) activity. Both types of processing are capable of being performed under operating software control (a supervisor or executive system) by taking advantage of the multiprogramming capability of the hardware and software.

Some organizations have developed or obtained a generalized data management system that is flexible enough to support the need of a wide variety of users. Such a system consists of a series of software programs that have the ability to create and update files, select, retrieve, and sort data, and generate reports. The generally accepted requirements for a system to be known as a data management system include the capability to create, revise, and delete records from a file, an interrogation or information retrieval capability that includes such features as sorting and limited computations, and finally a report-generating capability that can meet user-specified parameters. Additional characteristics may be added to the basic system depending on the capabilities of a specific hardware configuration. Teleprocessing and on-line inquiry capabilities are often added. The following basic elements can be identified as potential components of a data management system:

1. Data base management languages
   (a) Data definition language
   (b) Data manipulation language
2. Retrieval subsystem
   (a) Search routines
   (b) Extract routines
3. Processing subsystem
   (a) Data validation
   (b) Logic and arithmetic ability
   (c) Update ability
4. Output subsystem
   (a) Sort-merge
   (b) Report preparation
   (c) Display preparation
5. Communications subsystem
   (a) Terminal and line-handling capabilities
   (b) Resource allocation
6. Other elements
   (a) Data security
   (b) Restart and recovery

A data management system makes it possible for various applications to work with a common data base when the data base is an interrelated set of organization files. As discussed earlier in this chapter, three levels can be defined within the decision-making and data requirement hierarchy: (1) strategic planning, which is identified with policy management and is applied to determining long-range objectives, (2) management control, which is associated with middle management and the ongoing administration of the organization, and (3) operational control, which is normally associated with supervisors and foremen at the working level and is concerned with task performance. Data requirements differ with the level of user. Policy management will usually require summary reports in contrast to the greater detail required by middle management. The report formats requested by the user will vary with the user's level in the organization.

Another user classification identifies four levels of data management system users: the data base manager, the applications programmer, the specializer, and the general user. The data base manager initially sets up the data base and establishes a data structure to meet his needs and the needs of the other users. The applications programmer writes and is responsible for programs to operate on the data base.

The specializer would be the typical user of a data management system with a highly structured inquiry language that permits nontechnical personnel to make inquiries into or update the data base. This user could be either a manager or lower-level employee. The general user needs no knowledge of procedural programming, nor need he understand the data system language. All his requirements are predefined by a higher-level user, and he need only understand how to make the queries, not define them. Examples of this user are bank tellers and retail sales personnel.

The four-level classification—data base manager, applications programmer, specializer, and general user—also allows for different levels of users of a data management system with different demands for information. Each user must be able to address a common data base and receive correct information in the proper format.

The analysis of a business system has parallels in the analysis of living organisms. The biologist studies the structure, functions, classifications of organisms; the systems analyst studies the structure, functions, and classifications of business data systems. Living organisms react to an environment, grow, adapt to changes in the environment, and have a high level of organization. Business systems have the same characteristics. For either the living organism or the business system to operate effectively, it must be organized in and functionally adapted to a specific environment with which it interacts. Design failures in either the organism or business are disruptive or fatal.

The business system must, in an organic sense, interact with an external environment. The design goals of the data system will establish the logic by which the system receives input from the external environment, interprets the input, and then makes decisions that result in reports, inquiry responses, displays, or commands. Figure 2-3 illustrates a feedback model that can be modified to study either living organisms or business systems.

If the design goals are deficient, the business system that has been created will malfunction or fail. The system will not effectively respond to and operate in its environment. Users will become dissatis-

Figure 2-3. System feedback model.

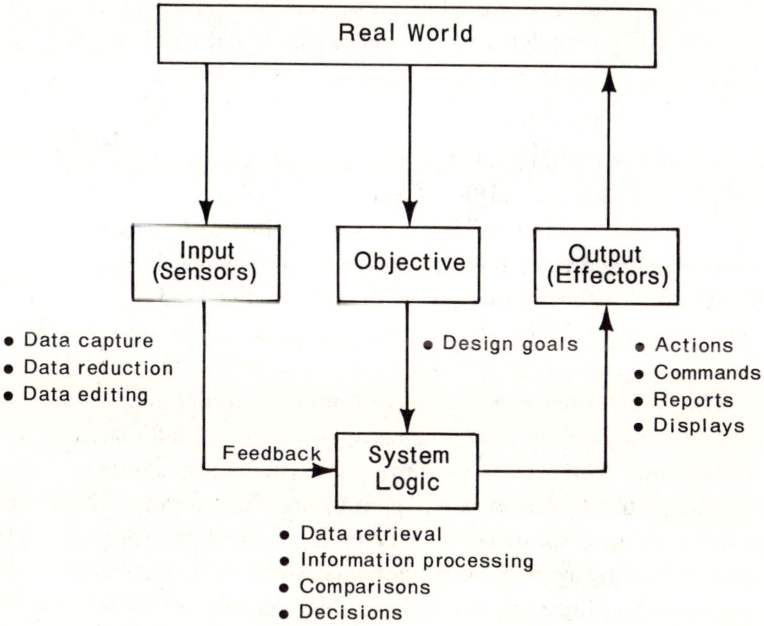

fied with the outputs from the system and seek alternatives to satisfy their information requirements.

A hierarchy can usually be established by the systems analyst during the design of a complex data system. A *system* consists of related activities that meet major company objectives such as inventory control or production scheduling. Figure 2-4 illustrates the information flow between major corporate systems. The activities that comprise those systems share a common data base and interact on common or related transaction data. A system can be automated, partially automated, or operated manually.

An inventory system would consist of activities that satisfy the corporate inventory control function by:

Maintaining stock levels
Minimizing inventory surpluses
Providing current, accurate inventory records
Avoiding shortages or production bottlenecks
Controlling inventory physical deterioration and obsolescence
Documenting usage trends
Flagging usage deviations

Sometimes it is desirable to divide an application into subsystems to simplify the information flow for analysis, evaluation, and design. A *subsystem* is a set of identifiable, related activities within a system. Systems often are divided into subsystems to simplify development or understanding of the components of the system. For example, an inventory system could be subdivided into three subsystems: ordering, forecasting, and reviewing.

The ordering subsystem would determine the economic order quantity based on inventory carrying costs, reorder costs, sales rate, and effective unit cost. The forecasting subsystem would establish the reorder point for each inventory item by analyzing historical inventory usage patterns to estimate future demands. Several analytical methods such as moving average, correlation analysis, and exponential smoothing could be utilized to determine reorder points.

Figure 2-4. Industrial information flow.

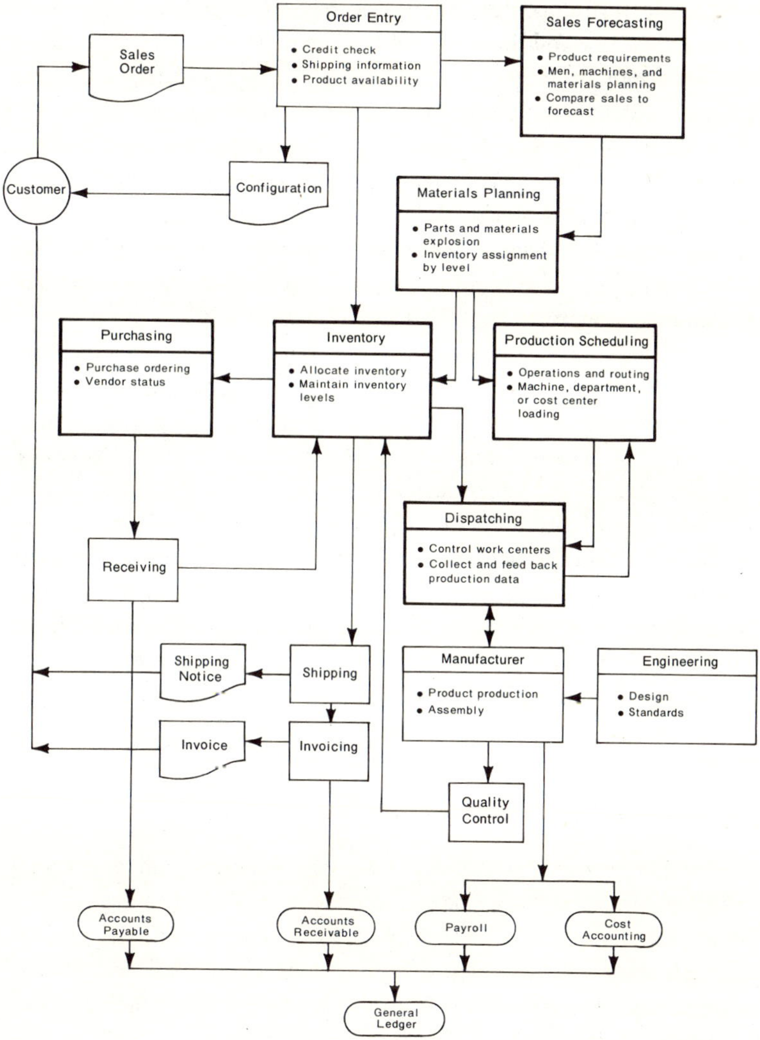

The reviewing subsystem would compare available stock with the order point established by the forecasting subsystem to ascertain whether the inventory item should be reordered. If the inventory of the item were low and there should be a reorder, the reviewing subsystem would look up the economic order quantity calculated by the ordering subsystem and initiate the reorder.

The three inventory subsystems—ordering, forecasting, and reviewing—could be further divided into processes. A *process* consists of a logical series of steps performed within a system or subsystem. Processes describe the detailed functions performed by the system, and they are studied by the systems analyst to determine whether they are suitable for automation.

For example, the ordering subsystem requires a logical inventory carrying cost that is found through a study of capital, taxes, storage, depreciation, spoilage, obsolescence, and insurance. A specific process or sequence of steps is required to gather basic source information and then calculate the inventory carrying cost.

Processes can be further subdivided into specific functions. A *function* consists of all the operations performed by a single organizational element at a single stage of a complex work cycle. An *operation* consists of all the related elements performed at one time by an individual in performing his or her work cycle. An *element* is a discrete work detail performed by an individual that is capable of definition and duplication.

SYSTEM ANALYSIS AND DESIGN SKILLS

The project management or systems analysis staff developing a data system must have specific management and technical skills. Unfortunately, there is a scarcity of senior managers and systems analysts with the following ones: project management, oral and written communication, research and analysis, data collection, systems analysis, systems design, and system documentation.

Project management skills include the ability to develop a project plan that establishes the project budget, budget controls, and estimated manpower requirements. After the project plan has been prepared, the manager must monitor the progress of the project against the time and cost milestones that have been established.

In setting up a project, the manager must be able to evaluate the proposed work scheduled and the staff skills and qualifications. That necessitates an understanding of the system requirements and design concept of a major data system involving both manual and automated processes.

Major projects should be planned with Gantt or PERT charts, and therefore the manager or analyst should be familiar with those project planning and control techniques. The project work progress will be compared with the plan as defined by the Gantt or PERT chart.

Oral and written communication skills include the capability to instruct project team members and give oral presentations to policy management. The project manager must be able to define and express work assignments and project objectives clearly. He must also be able to communicate effectively with team members in order to identify problems related to individuals, attitudes, assignments, and work progress.

Although the need for effective communication is obvious, a surprising number of problems that impede the design and implementation of data systems relate to poor communications. Too often, ambiguous work assignments are made or major problems are buried until they delay or destroy the planned data system.

Communications skills also include the ability to listen. Good listening by project management opens communication channels upward and keeps management informed as to people and technical problems. Effective listening, like effective oral communication, is a skill.

Policy and middle management should be briefed on the benefits to be derived from and the requirements for the successful implementation of data systems. The communications process is necessary to define the system requirements of policy and middle management properly and to win the cooperation and support of managers on those levels. Too often, data systems are designed without adequate input from or the understanding and support of user management.

The project manager and systems analysts must be capable of interviewing user management to document viewpoints, needs, and concerns. Interviewing skills are vital to the proper definition of user requirements, although they seldom receive enough emphasis when profiles of desirable systems analyst skills and training are prepared.

Finally, the project manager and analysts should be able to write and edit the technical papers and manuals necessary to control and document the development of a data system. That includes the ability to rewrite technical documents in order to upgrade quality and content.

Research and analysis requires a review of the general and technical literature related to a data system to obtain information and define constraints. For example, the desire of management to develop a data system may be based upon previous surveys, reports, and committee and task force meetings. The project manager and systems analyst staff must be able to review and analyze the existing background material to familiarize themselves with the history of a project.

In addition, the development of a data system may require research into general and technical publications to obtain information about an application, similar applications that have been automated, information system design principles, or computer hardware and software capabilities. The individual conducting that research must be able to organize and then conduct a research study.

The research process requires taking notes, organizing and synthesizing information, and summarizing conclusions into organized report form. Often a substantial body of existing reports and literature must be studied and the significant contents reduced to summary report form.

Data collection involves designing interview guides and data collection forms and writing complete and clear instructions for the completion of the forms. The analyst should develop a method for distributing and collecting the forms, and he should also conduct actual data collection interviews.

Two types of interviews are commonly used by analysts; they are called structured and general interviews. A structured interview is guided by a set of predefined questions. It is normally used when several people with similar or related positions are to be interviewed individually or in small groups in an attempt to arrive at a set of conclusions. A general interview is less formal and more flexible than a structured one. The session format and direction will vary greatly with the personalities of the interviewer and the interviewee.

The need for analysts to be trained in data collection methodology and trained to conduct data-gathering interviews is not adequately stressed. Numerous data system projects have been crippled by faulty data collection forms and interviewing techniques. Failures in information gathering result in improperly designed systems that cannot respond to user requirements. The quality of the design specifications for a data system varies directly with the skill of the project team in collecting accurate and relevant information.

Systems analysis requires the organization and summarization of collected data, the analysis and description of major and minor work processes, and the construction, if appropriate, of flow process charts or decision table models. The analyst constructs a quantitative model of the existing system and may use statistical procedures to study the data that have been collected.

During the systems analysis task, the analyst will identify illogical sequences, unnecessary operations, and duplicative operations in the existing system. Next he will study alternative systems or methods that utilize personnel, equipment, or programs more efficiently. He will then construct descriptive and quantitative models of the alternate systems and compare them with the existing system.

In his *systems design* role, the systems analyst devises the structure of a new automated data system and defines the functions of its components. He identifies the main subsystems comprising a system and indicates the relation between the subsystems. He also evaluates alternate methods for each function within a work process.

Each subsystem, process, function, and operation is defined in terms of utility and purpose. The specific action steps, input information, decision logic, output reports, and output routing are described in detail for each process in the system. Forms and reports are drawn by the analyst, and instruction manuals are prepared. Job aids, interchange codes, convention, and interface requirements are defined. The list of tasks and executive decisions required to build the system is specified, and system test and control procedures are developed.

The *system documentation* skills of the analyst involve the writing or evaluation of user documents describing the data system and the presentation of oral reports to users and management. The programming staff receives the system design specifications from the systems analyst staff and flow-charts the logic of programs, writes programs, and completes program and system testing. The tested operational system is then turned over to the operations staff for live production and system maintenance.

SYSTEM DEVELOPMENT STEPS

The development of a data system requires a specific sequence of steps: initiation, analysis, design, development, implementation, and operation.

During the *initiation phase* of a project, a user recognizes a need for data processing services, states that need, and, hopefully, receives a proposal for the work to be accomplished. The statement of need may be followed by a feasibility study the purpose of which is to determine whether the benefits to be derived from a proposed new system offset the development cost. If the feasibility study results are favorable, there is usually a progression to detailed system development.

A project plan should be developed to control the project. It should describe the activities comprising the project and also their interrelation. The project manager should assign a schedule, manpower, and miscellaneous costs to each planned project activity.

During the *analysis phase* of a project, the old system, if there is one, is studied and a functional description is prepared to define in user terms the capabilities and benefits of the system to be developed. The functional description, written in user language, should be formally approved by the user prior to detailed work.

In the *design phase* of a project, detailed specifications for the new system are prepared. System flow charts are prepared; the data base structure is defined; all input/output is defined; and detailed program specifications are written. This information is collected and published in a systems design report. For larger systems, the system/subsystem, data base, and program specifications might be separately bound rather than be contained in a single systems design report.

During *development*, programmers work directly from the detailed design specifications, and those specifications are translated into computer programs. This involves logic flow-charting, program coding, compilation, and the testing and debugging of programs.

During *implementation*, system testing is completed and conversion to the new system is accomplished. The programs that have been written are run as a system to insure that program and system interfaces have been properly defined and tested. Data conversion and user training also are completed. If an old system exists, a parallel run of the old and new systems may be made to compare the outputs of the two systems.

After testing and conversion, the new system begins live *operation* and a postconversion evaluation is made of its effectiveness. It is evaluated relative to the functional description and detailed design specifications. It is also maintained in that system modifications are made to satisfy user requests.

DOCUMENT TYPES

A number of different documents will be produced in the development of a data system. Each document will be written for a specific reader and, therefore, the documents will greatly differ in tone and structure. This chapter defines sixteen documents that may be produced during the design and development of a computer application. They have been listed sequentially, as used in each step.

Initiation Stage

- The *user request* (UR) is the user document requesting data processing services. This document, for example, describes in general terms the output of a desired computer application.
- The *user proposal* (UP) is the proposal from the data center or contractor prepared to satisfy the user request.
- The *feasibility study* (FS) is undertaken to determine whether the benefits to be derived from a proposed new system justify the development time and cost.
- The *project plan* (PP) defines the tasks comprising a project, makes personnel assignments, assigns time schedules, establishes review points or milestones, and estimates development costs.

Analysis Stage

- The *functional description* (FD) results from systems analysis. It is a technical document that defines in user language the system to be developed. The user should review it and request changes in it prior to detailed system development.
- A *data requirements document* (DR) may be developed to list and define data elements that the system must handle and specify data collection requirements to the user.

Design Stage

- The *system/subsystem specifications* (SS) define the logical components of the system to be developed.
- The *data base specifications* (DS) define the structure, contents, and operational characteristics of the system data base.
- The *program specifications* (PS) define the requirements and characteristics of each computer program to be developed.

Development

- The *program documentation* (PD) consists of the logic flow charts and narrative descriptions supporting each program that has been developed.

Implementation

- The *test and implementation plan* (TP) specifies the sequence of steps and materials necessary to test the system prior to live operation.
- The *test analysis report* (TA) describes the condition of the system and programs after testing.
- The *user manual* (UM) describes the system to the user. The manual indicates to the user how to provide input to the system effectively and how to interpret output reports from the system.

Operation

- The *operations manual* (OM) contains the information and procedures necessary to operate the computer system that has been developed. It is directed toward the computer operations people who will actually run the system.
- The *maintenance manual* (MM) contains specific information on each computer program. Its purpose is to permit the maintenance of the system in terms of changes and modifications.
- The *evaluation report* (ER) is prepared after a system becomes operational and indicates whether the operational system is meeting design specifications.

PROJECT DOCUMENTATION

The project documentation is the record of system development; it is the primary reference for system review or modification. Figure 2-5 shows the distribution of the correspondence, charts, specification, manuals, and other materials created as a result of the work completed to comply with a user request for service. The logical components of that project documentation are project, systems, program, production, and user folders. The systems, program, and production folders will normally reside in a central documentation library with a controlled circulation. The project folder will usually be maintained in the office of the director of data processing. The user folder will be located in the office of the user.

The project folder, in historical sequence, contains a record of user correspondence and management control information relating to a project. The project plan contained in this folder is the primary refer-

Figure 2-5. Project documentation.

PROJECT FOLDER
- Correspondence
- User Request (UR)
- User Proposal (UP)
- Project Plan (PP)

SYSTEMS FOLDER
- Feasibility Study (FS)
- Functional Description (FD)
- Data Requirements Document (DR)
- Detail Design Report
  - System/Subsystem Specifications (SS)
  - Data Base Specifications (DS)
  - Program Specifications (PS)
- Test and Implementation Plan (TP)
- Evaluation Report (ER)

PROGRAM FOLDER
- Program Documentation (PD)
- Test Analysis Report (TA)

PRODUCTION FOLDER
- Operations Manual (OM)
- Maintenance Manual (MM)

USER FOLDER
- User Manual (UM)

ence point to monitor project progress and the utilization of the manpower, time, and machine resources.

The systems folder contains the record of systems analysis and design work completed during the project. Included are the functional description, the system/subsystem specifications, data base specifications, program specifications, and test and implementation plan. A copy of the evaluation report comparing live system operation with design specifications is also contained in the folder.

The program documentation and a copy of the system test analysis report are contained in the program folder. This part of the program documentation includes block diagrams, program listings, program test results, and similar information necessary to understand and maintain computer programs.

The production folder contains the operations manual and the maintenance manual. The operations manual contains the instructions necessary to schedule, initiate, process, and control all the jobs of a system in a production state. That includes job flow charts, job-initiating instructions, production schedules, and similar information. The maintenance manual describes the maintenance requirements of the system.

The user folder contains the user manual and related user training materials. It also contains instructional material for user personnel describing user responsibilities and procedures relative to the proper entry of data into the system and interpretation of output reports.

MANAGEMENT OPTIONS

Not all the documents described in the section Document Types may be required for a particular project. Typically, on a small project, documents will run together. For example, the user, operations, and maintenance documents may be contained in one manual. The project manager, after determining project size and complexity, must on that basis decide which documents will be required for the project. Figure 2-6 shows the relation between document types and project types. A data center will typically work with the following types of projects, and the documentation requirements will vary accordingly:

I. A *feasibility study* would require an investigation into the feasibility of a proposed data system.

II. The *new system* (*no manual system*) type of project requires the development of a data system that will perform functions that have not previously been performed manually.

III. The *new system* type of project involves the automation of business functions that are performed manually.

IV. A *complex system modification* would require a modification of or change to an existing data system and a substantial work effort.

V. *Simple system modification* would require relatively minor modification of an operational data system.

VI. *Emergency program maintenance* requires the performance of emergency maintenance work such as making a patch to an operational data system.

Figure 2-6. System type and documentation requirements.

SYSTEM TYPE	UR	UP	FS	PP	FD	DR	SS	DS	PS	PD	TP	TA	UM	OM	MM	ER
I. Feasibility study	X	X	X	X												
II. New system (no manual system)	X	X	X	X	X	X	X	X	X	X	X	X	X	X	X	X
III. New system	X	X	X	X	X	X	X	X	X	X	X	X	X	X	X	X
IV. Complex system modification	X	X	X	X	X	X	X	X	X	X	X	X	X	X	X	X
V. Simple system modification	X	X	X	X	X	X	X	X	X	X	X	X	X	X	X	X
VI. Emergency maintenance										X	X	X	X			

SUMMARY

Early computer systems were installed primarily to automate accounting applications that were already semiautomated. By the late 1960s, however, their role had been expanded to support major production, marketing, and personnel functions.

The management functions that can be supported by data systems are strategic planning, management control, and operational control. The strategic planning role involves the selection of corporate objectives and the policies and resources necessary to achieve the defined objectives. The management control role, exercised by middle management, requires the effective deployment and utilization of resources to attain the objectives. The operational control role insures that specific tasks are accomplished.

Data systems can operate in either a batch or an on-line mode. Batch systems run in a time-dependent or sequential manner in contrast to on-line systems, which utilize terminals to deliver information directly to management. Real-time systems perform a computation during the actual time in which a physical process transpires, and that computation influences the outcome of the physical process.

Some organizations are utilizing data management systems that are flexible enough to support a variety of users. The generally accepted requirements for a system to be known as a data management system include the capability to create, revise, and delete records from a file, an interrogation or information retrieval capability that includes such features as sorting and limited computations, and, finally, a report-generating capability that can meet user-specified parameters. Teleprocessing and on-line inquiry capabilities are often added to a data management system.

An analogy can be made between the biologist studying living organisms and the systems analyst designing a data system. The biologist studies the structure, functions, and classifications of organisms; the systems analyst similarly studies the structure, functions, and classifications of business data systems. The following terms apply to the design of data systems:

System. Related activities meeting a major objective.
Subsystem. A component of a system consisting of related activities.
Process. A series of functional steps within a system or subsystem.
Function. A number of operations performed at a stage in a work cycle.
Operation. Related work elements performed by an individual.
Element. A discrete work detail performed by an individual.

The project management or systems analysis staff developing a data system should possess the following qualifications:

Project management
Oral and written communication
Research and analysis
Data collection
Systems analysis
Systems design
System documentation

The development of a data system involves six basic steps: initiation, analysis, design, development, implementation, and operation. Sixteen documents can be produced during the design and development of a computer application:

User Request (UR)
User Proposal (UP)
Feasibility Study (FS)
Project Plan (PP)
Functional Description (FD)
Data Requirements Document (DR)
System/Subsystem Specifications (SS)
Data Base Specifications (DS)
Program Specifications (PS)

Program Documentation (PD)
Test and Implementation Plan (TP)
Test Analysis Report (TA)
User Manual (UM)
Operations Manual (OM)
Maintenance Manual (MM)
Evaluation Report (ER)

Those sixteen documents are filed in five basic document folders: project, systems, program, production, and user. Documentation requirements will vary with the size and complexity of a specific project. Typically, on a small project several document types will be combined in one volume.

3. Initiation

This chapter discusses the start of an information system project. The decisions and responsibilities of policy and middle management are defined, and key documents required by user management to define the scope and cost of a developmental effort are discussed. The data processing manager is provided with a framework for the control of project time and cost.

During the initial phase of a project prior to development work, a user request is defined and a user proposal is submitted to service that request. If the proposal is accepted by the user, a detailed project plan for the work to be accomplished should be prepared. The plan should indicate personnel, time, and other resources required to complete the project. Sometimes a feasibility study is authorized to determine the benefits and cost effectiveness of the proposed system relative to developmental time and cost.

USER REQUEST (UR)

A user request for service is shown in Figure 3-1. User requests may be made orally, but eventually they must be written.

Oral requests without documentation usually lead to misunderstandings between the user and the data processing staff. *The user should briefly describe the computer application or other service desired on a simple form.*

A request for service may come from any level in the firm. The education of users will improve the ability of the user to translate his needs into a form meaningful to the data processing analyst. Training of systems analysts in corporate operations also simplifies the translation.

Figure 3-1. User request form.

User Request Form

Date:

Requesting Department

Requested by:

Name ____________________

Title ____________________

Phone ____________________

Project Work Request and Description:

USER PROPOSAL (UP)

An example of a user proposal is shown in Figure 3-2. The analyst assigned to investigate the user request should schedule a meeting with the user. This meeting should be an exploratory one to review the scope of the proposed work, interfaces with related projects and systems, and the user benefits to be derived from the project.

Figure 3-2. User proposal.

	System Type Inventory System
From: Data Processing Director	Preliminary Estimate ☒
To: Client Department	Final Estimate ☐

I. DEVELOPMENTAL COSTS AND SCHEDULE

	Major Project Activities		*Estimated Costs*	*Start Date*	*Completion Date*
(1)	Initiation		$ 1,550	1/15	1/31
(2)	Analysis		11,200	2/1	3/15
(3)	Design		28,425	3/16	4/30
(4)	Development (programming)		43,100	5/1	7/31
(5)	Implementation		11,725	8/1	9/15
	A. System testing	$7,500			
	B. User training	4,225			
(6)	Operation		4,125	9/16	10/31
	A. Production turnover	2,550			
	B. System evaluation	1,575			
(7)	Other (travel)		925		
			Estimated Developmental Costs		$101,050

II. ANNUAL OPERATING COSTS

	Requirements	*Estimated Costs*
(1)	Computer time	$16,400
(2)	Data conversion	8,115
(3)	System maintenance	5,200
(4)	Other	
	Estimated Operating Costs	$29,715

Time frames for accomplishment of user objectives should be discussed and agreed upon. At this time, the expected degree of involvement of user personnel in the project should be defined. Further meetings should be scheduled if more information is required by the analyst before a proposal can be prepared for the user. After the initial discussions, the project analyst should prepare a proposal for the user.

The user proposal should contain a brief description of the project and the objectives to be achieved. The responsibilities of user personnel should be defined, and the number and level of personnel that the user must assign to the project should be indicated. A final date for acceptance of the proposal by the user should be specified.

The major project tasks and user costs should be outlined as shown in Figure 3–2. The estimation of the time and cost necessary to develop data processing applications requires consideration of a number of factors. A key element in accurate time and cost estimating is the division of large systems and programming efforts into a number of activities to each of which a time and cost can be assigned. The work tasks defined by the analyst may include a feasibility study in addition to systems design and programming or may specify only programming tasks.

A major developmental project will include the primary six phases discussed in Chapter 2 and indicate a developmental schedule and cost for each phase. These phases—initiation, analysis, design, development, implementation, and operation—should be subdivided, if appropriate, into subtasks.

In addition to developmental costs, the proposal should indicate, as shown in Figure 3–2, the annual system operating costs. The user should be informed as to the computer time, data conversion personnel, and other resources required to operate and maintain the system after it has been developed.

Data processing costs can be segregated into two major categories, nonrecurring and recurring. Nonrecurring costs include the investment in preparing a computer facility, the initial systems effort preceding the installation of the computer, the cost of converting the company's existing data files onto the media required by the computer system, the costs of parallel running of systems as the new system is introduced, and the cost of system testing and debugging to insure that the new system operates correctly.

Recurring costs are continuing costs for equipment, personnel, and facilities after the data system is operational. Operating costs, which also are recurring, include the salaries of operators, the cost of supplies, and the power and air conditioning necessary to keep the equipment operating.

The proposal might also contain a brief description of project staffing and organization. Included in the narrative would be the project organization and the general number and level of competence of people to be assigned at each level. If different phases require different types of staffing, that should be specified.

If the user accepts the proposal, a simple letter saying so should be sent to the data processing director. An account and project identification number is then assigned to the project for control and billing purposes.

FEASIBILITY STUDY (FS)

Sometimes a systems analyst will be unable to define a data system without additional study and will therefore recommend that a feasibility study be conducted. Such a study requires careful planning and a well-defined approach and methodology. Typically, a feasibility study report has the following content:

1. Objectives and background
   - Purpose of the feasibility study
   - Project references
2. Study recommendations
   - Summary of findings
   - Alternatives considered
   - Study recommendations

3. Proposed system
   System benefits
   Relation to existing systems
   Effect on current operations
4. Action plan
   Decisions required
   Schedule of activities
   Resources required

OBJECTIVES AND BACKGROUND

The primary purpose of the feasibility study is to determine whether the value and benefits of a new system justify the cost to develop and operate the system. The study will undertake to examine existing data processing operations and determine the benefits, if any, to be derived from automation. *It should be objective and not become a rubber stamp of someone's opinion or recommendation.* It should also recognize that some processes and operations should not be automated. Too often, applications are automated without adequate analysis or cost justification.

The time and resources needed for a substantive feasibility study as well as the importance of the study are frequently underestimated. The report should contain a concise statement of conclusions and recommendations, as well as material supporting the study findings. The statement of conclusions and recommendations should include a breakdown of cost information describing the present and proposed systems, the major resources required to develop and operate the proposed system, and an analysis of the benefits and cost effectiveness of the proposed system. The study also indicates, if development is recommended, a tentative time schedule for key decisions and work activities.

The communication of study plans to employees is a management responsibility that is often not given sufficient attention. Management's support of the study should be communicated to company personnel. The initiation of a feasibility study may alarm the staff and working forces because of the possibility of job reassignments or of machines replacing people. Employees should be informed in order to obtain their cooperation and reduce the possibility of resistance to change.

Top management participation in setting the ground rules for the feasibility study should also include the establishment of basic objectives. The study purpose should be stated precisely; areas for inclusion or exclusion should be defined; and depth of analysis should be planned.

A careful plan of action that reflects both the views of management and those of the technical study team should be prepared. An approved plan of action is important because the study may cut across organizational lines and lead to recommended changes in procedures, organization, and information flow. The charter for the study should define responsibilities and assign adequate authority, staff, and resources.

STUDY RECOMMENDATIONS

The initial step of the feasibility study is to determine the organizational framework of the activity being studied. Legal statutes, policy directives, and managerial restrictions define the organizational framework.

The organizational structure being studied should be charted. Major elements to identify are company, division, branch, department, unit, and subunit. A chart should also be obtained or prepared to show the grade or rank of the personnel affected by the study.

Study interviews usually start with the top levels of management and progress downward through middle management and individual office and factory personnel. The systems analyst should attempt to establish working relations with people he interviews during this study phase. Interviews should be planned to avoid wasting people's time with irrelevant questions, and interview sessions should not be overly long.

After the user interviews, the systems analyst selects for investigation the operations that are likely to derive the greatest benefits from the use of new procedures and equipment. He should study those areas in detail to determine whether they merit using advanced data processing methods. Usually, the impetus for the feasibility study will have been a particular operating situation that is affecting costs and company profits. Thus, the starting point is the study of current systems and an analysis of where they fail to meet business objectives.

Major benefits that companies have derived from automation are:

Information and reports that were previously unavailable can be obtained.

Information and reports can be obtained on a more timely basis.

The business process or operation is improved.

Mathematical calculations are made more rapidly or accurately.

Clerical costs are reduced or avoided.

Management decision making is improved.

The company's competitive position is strengthened.

The image of the company to customers is improved.

Internal bottlenecks are reduced or eliminated and employee morale is thereby improved.

To identify prime areas for analysis, it is useful to consider the following items:

Responsibilities of the organization being studied.

Source data generated and handled and the volume of the data.

Quality control editing performed on the source data.

Files maintained by the organization and file sizes.

Number, content, and frequency of reports produced by or for the organization.

Frequency of report preparation.

Adequacy of information contained in reports.

Justification of frequency of report preparation.

Satisfaction with timeliness, reliability, and utility of existing system.

Plans for automation or system redesign.
The organization's current staffing levels and job descriptions.
Any data processing currently being performed for the organization.
New requirements or responsibilities anticipated by the organization.

High-volume operations or repetitive operations with high clerical costs lend themselves to automation. Some of the characteristics of a process or operation that may justify automation are:

High transaction volumes (inventory, sales, purchase orders).
Repetitive transactions (high volume with a repetition of procedures such as payroll transactions).
Complex calculations (work routing and machine scheduling).
Common source documents (the utilization of information on a common source document by many processes or operations).
Response time required (need for rapid inquiry response processing such as airline reservations and banking transactions).

An important consideration is the relation between systems. Thc systems in an organization may be either independent or interdependent. For example, inventory control is essentially independent of personnel records, but it is closely related to production control. System relations have an important bearing on plans for automation in that boundaries between systems and interfaces must be defined. Separate organizational units may depend upon common data or common information files.

The detailed analysis of specific business systems includes obtaining complete information about the existing systems from both internal and external sources. The objective is to relate the operation being studied to a larger production or administrative process or system. Facts about the internal functioning of the system should be collected or cataloged. Information will be gathered by interviewing key personnel, collecting working documents, and estimating and sampling.

The systems analyst performs an analysis of existing operations and explores alternative methods and procedures; he considers the possibility of eliminating basic and intermediate work elements or operations. Analysis may show that specific data are no longer needed or that vital information is not available. Useful aids for analysis are flow charts, workload profiles, time schedules, process flow charts, and procedure manuals. In evaluating a proposed system, the costs and benefits must be compared with those of the present system. The present system is always used as the basis for evaluating the proposed system.

PROPOSED SYSTEM

The benefits from data systems can be tangible or intangible. A tangible benefit can be related directly to a cost savings or system improvement; an intangible benefit cannot be. An example of an intangible benefit is an improvement in customer service obtained from a more responsive order-processing system. Even though the improvement is a result of the new system, it is difficult to place a monetary value on it. Some benefits are more tangible than others, but a new system may be justified by intangible benefits.

The figures that form the foundation for the feasibility report are separated into recurring and nonrecurring costs and tangible and intangible benefits. Those figures are used in a return-on-investment (ROI) calculation:

$$\text{Return on investment} = \frac{\text{tangible benefits} - \text{recurring cost}}{\text{nonrecurring costs}}$$

Note that only tangible benefits are included in the calculation. Each figure must be backed up by a thorough analysis and must be a logical outgrowth of the facts obtained during the feasibility study. The basis of systems evaluation is the appraisal of the costs and benefits of alternative systems. At the end of the analysis, the study team will have answered the question whether it is economically desirable for the company to automate the system.

ACTION PLAN

The final task for the analysts of the existing system is to organize and present the results to management. The written report should contain a concise statement of conclusions and recommendations as well as supporting material for the study. The statement of conclusions should include a breakdown of cost figures for the present and proposed systems, the major resource requirements of the proposed system, an explanation of benefits, and the rationale of the recommendations. The report, if appropriate, should contain the tentative timetable for proceeding with the preparation of functional specifications. Sufficient detail should be included to permit a management decision on whether to proceed with the data system. The appendix should contain more detailed documentation of the activities of the business such as operation sheets and preliminary reports to management.

PROJECT PLAN (PP)

After a user authorization to conduct a feasibility study or implement a system has been received, the assigned project manager should plan in more detail the work to be accomplished. A major data processing management problem is control of application development time and cost.

Successful project management requires that a project plan and structure be defined at project inception. The project, if it is large enough, should be broken down into subunits or modules. The subunits should then be analyzed to establish the checkpoints or milestones necessary for management control. If possible, each milestone should have a visible output, a document or product, that clearly establishes the status and quality of work that has been performed on the project at that particular point in the development cycle.

Project control requires control of quality, cost, time, and resources. Basically, we are seeking to answer with a project control system the following questions:

Cost

- What will total estimated project costs be?
- Is the actual project cost to date over or under cost estimates?

Time

- What is the estimated time to complete the total project?
- Is the project ahead of or behind schedule?
- When should each activity start?
- What will happen to the project if the completion of an activity is ahead of or behind schedule?

Resources

- How many people should be assigned to the project?
- What skills should the assigned people have?
- How should specific work assignments be made?
- What machine time and other resources are required by the project?

Bar charts and network planning methods provide the methodology for the division of work into discrete activities. In considering the time and manpower resources that must be assigned to each activity, the following factors should be considered:

The work experience and general capabilities of the analysis and programming personnel who can be assigned to the work.

The magnitude of effort in terms of manpower and other resources required to complete the particular activity.

The programming language chosen for application programming. Higher-level languages such as COBOL and FORTRAN usually require less programming time than assembly languages.

The logical structuring, file accessing, and updating complexity of the system data base.

The number of different types of input documents and output reports to be processed by the system.

The degree of system specifications change expected during system development.

The unique requirements of an on-line system, which must be considered in estimating time and cost requirements if the system to be developed will operate in an on-line mode.

After a user authorization to implement has been received by the data center, the project manager should assign a schedule, manpower allocation, miscellaneous costs, and operations costs to each planned activity by utilizing a project plan form an example of which is illustrated in Figure 3-3. After the *project plan* has been approved, work on the project can commence.

The project manager is responsible for the successful completion of the project. He will initially develop the project plan that contains a description of all the activities comprising the project and their interrelations. As part of that plan, he will have estimated the manpower, machine, and other resources necessary to complete the project effectively. He will also develop a list of milestone review points against which to measure project progress.

Project quantitative control involves a comparison of budgeted versus actual manpower, machine, and cost expenditures. Actual project progress at milestone points is compared with estimated progress to determine whether a project is on schedule. The project control system should provide the information necessary to control projects quantitatively. Project qualitative control includes review of the accuracy, completeness, and overall quality of the work performed. The project manager is responsible for the qualitative review.

Bar charts or CPM/PERT techniques, shown in Figures 3-4 and 3-5, can be utilized to plan and control project activities. The techniques provide a graphic representation, or model, of a project and a means of describing the interrelation between project tasks and separating the functions of planning and scheduling. *Planning* is defined as the act of stating the activities that must occur in a project and the order in which those activities are to be accomplished. Only technol-

Figure 3-3. Project plan.

Project Title: Equipment Maintenance System

Project Manager: R. Hyer

System Type: II

Date: 1/2

ACTIVITY		TIME SCHEDULE		MANPOWER ALLOCATION		COSTS		
Identification	Description	Start	Complete	Category	Hours	Cost Code	Description	Cost
001-002	Equipment Numbering	1/5	1/19	03	80	21	Travel	$100.00
001-003	Input Layouts	1/5	2/2	03	160	25	Supplies	$300.00
001-004	Conversion Plan	1/5	1/19	03	80			
002-006	Equipment Tagging	1/19	2/9	03	120			
003-005	Output Layouts	2/2	2/16	03	80			
005-006	File Design	2/16	3/29	03	240			
004-006	Test Plan	1/19	2/2	03	80			

ogy and sequence are considered. *Scheduling* is defined as the act of producing project timetables based on a plan and the costs and duration times associated with each activity. The analysis techniques of Figures 3-4 and 3-5 were developed to provide quantitative information for use in scheduling a project and as the basis of a system for management by exception.

The primary advantage of the bar chart is that it provides a simple, graphic means of portraying the plan, schedule, and progress of a project. A bar chart is particularly effective in showing the status of the various project activities. One can note the last posting date, draw a vertical line across the chart, and at once see which activities are behind or ahead of schedule. The following steps are necessary to prepare a bar chart.

Figure 3-4. Bar chart.

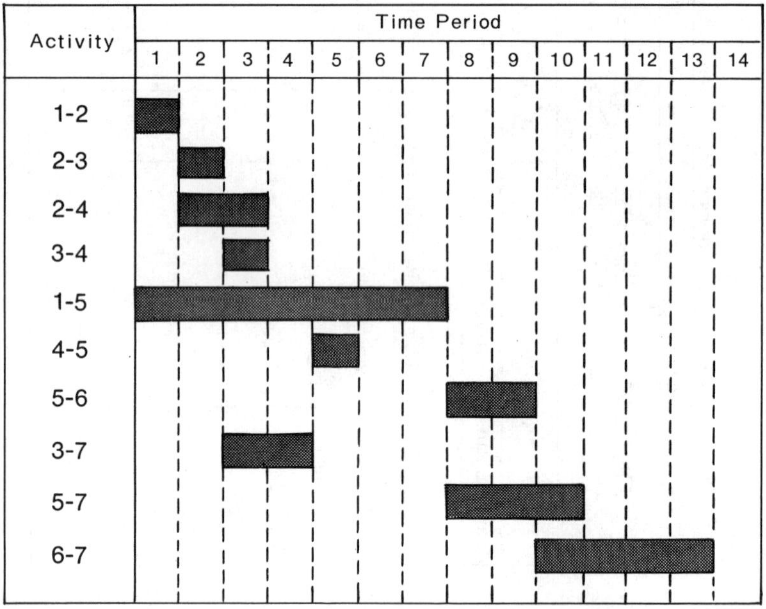

Figure 3-5. CPM network.

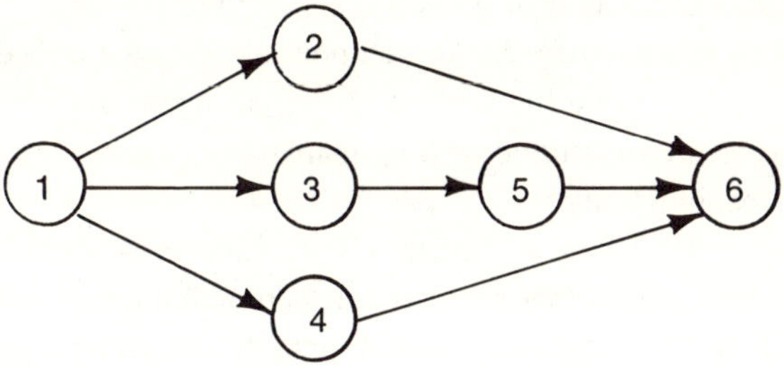

Activity	Duration (Weeks)	Start Time		Completion Time		Activity Slack
		Earliest	Latest	Earliest	Latest	
1-2	2	0	7	2	9	7
1-3	4	0	0	4	4	0
1-4	2	0	8	2	10	8
2-6	3	2	9	5	12	7
3-5	2	4	4	6	6	0
5-6	6	6	6	12	12	0
4-6	2	2	10	4	12	8

- Analyze the project and break it down into activities to be scheduled.
- Estimate the time required to perform each activity. The time estimate should be made by the individual who will perform the activity or after discussions with him or her.
- Arrange the project activity in the chart. List the activities on the left-hand side of the chart; they can be sequenced by working backward from the scheduled completion date.

A critical path network is also a graphical representation of a project and a means of describing the interrelation between project tasks and separating the functions of planning and scheduling. The following steps are necessary to prepare a critical path network:

- List all project activities.
- Assign a sequential number to each activity.
- Next to each activity list the sequential numbers of the activities that must precede the starting of the particular activity.
- Indicate the individual or the organizational entity that will perform each activity.
- Draw a network, as illustrated in Figure 3–5, to show the predecessor/successor relation between activities.
- Study the network to discover activity interrelations not previously considered.
- Select a project start date and assign a time duration to each activity.
- Compute the earliest and latest start and completion times of each activity. Networks of 100 or fewer activities can be calculated manually without difficulty. Computer processing should be employed for larger networks. To prepare a network manually, start with the first activity and work forward to compute the earliest start date for each activity. Next, work backward from the project completion date to compute the latest completion date for each activity.

The activities for which the earliest and latest start dates are the same are on the critical path, and the critical path activities determine the earliest date for project completion. Any slippage in the schedule for completion of critical path activities can delay the entire project.

The project control system must have an accounting feature that records the expenditure of manpower, machine, and other resources. The system illustrated in Figure 3-6 should record information on manpower and equipment utilization, miscellaneous expenses, and the status of the activity. It should permit the project manager to monitor the rate at which resources are being expended. He can then relate resource consumption to the estimates in the project plan.

The following reports are representative of those that can be utilized in a project control system.

Figure 3-6. Project accounting system.

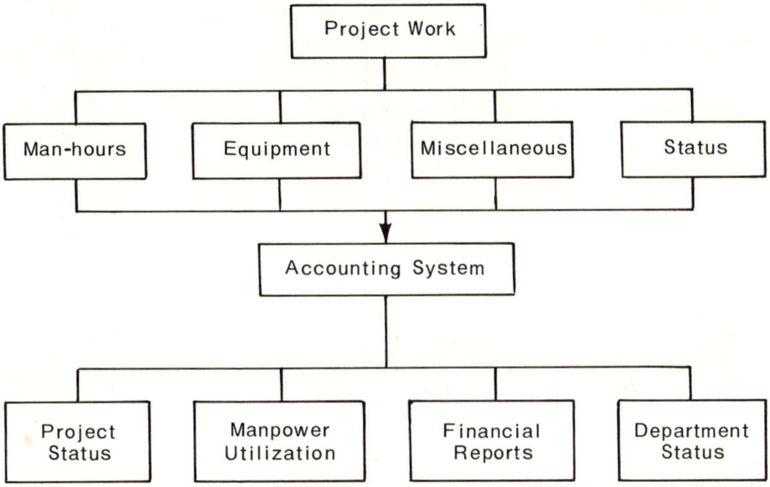

The *project activity report,* illustrated in Figure 3-7, goes to project leaders and management. It supplies estimated and actual time and cost expenditures by project activity.

The *production by employee report,* shown in Figure 3-8, shows the projects worked on, the kind of work done, and the number of hours by employee.

The *summary project progress report* lists projects and shows the original project cost estimates and actual expenditures to date.

The *employee production by work code report* provides information on the expenditure of manpower resources by type of work.

The accounting system will require that a set of codes and chart of accounts be specified to record and report resource consumption. The codes should identify resources expended by type and project. The following information should be captured and fed into the accounting system:

Project/activity
Employee identification

Figure 3-7. Project activity report.

Report Date 4/1

Project Name: *Equipment Maintenance System*
Project Leader: *R. Hyer*

	MAN-HOURS						MISCELLANEOUS COST				
		Estimated		Actual			Estimated		Actual to Date		
Activity	Scheduled Completion	Hours	Work Code	Hours	Work Code	Variance to Date (Hours)	Cost Code	Cost	Cost Code	Cost	Variance to Date ($)
001–002	1/19	80	03	80	03	0	21	$100.00	21	$ 50.00	$50.00
001–003	2/2	160	03	180	03	20	25	$300.00	25	$300.00	0
001–004	1/19	80	03	90	03	10					
002–006	2/9	120	03	120	03	0					
003–005	2/16	80	03	100	03	20					
005–006	3/29	240	03	240	03	0					
004–006	2/2	80	03	80	03	0					

Figure 3-8. Production by employee report.

EMPLOYEE NUMBER	EMPLOYEE	PROJECT NAME	CODE	HOURS
015	Mike Arnold	Payroll update	10	10
		Payroll update	12	12
		On-line personnel	10	10
		On-line personnel	16	3
		Total billable hours		35
		Total unbillable hours		5
022	Joan Arthur	Data base generation	11	20
		Inventory maintenance	13	10
		Total billable hours		30
		Total unbillable hours		10

Month/day/year
Work code/cost code
Number of chargeable units

Manpower costs represent a major component of most data system developmental projects. In order to compare actual manpower utilization on project activities with estimated utilization, data are usually collected from employees on weekly time sheets and put into the accounting system. The time sheet is usually prepared weekly by the employee, and it indicates, by day, the projects on which the employee has worked and the tasks he has performed. The time sheet should also indicate travel, training, and leave time.

A second major resource category is equipment or machine time. The job accounting software contained in the operating system can record computer processing time, storage space, job priority level, and similar information by user or project identification number. Each testing or production computer run can be identified by header information, and charges can be accumulated by billing number. Similar usage and billing information can be recorded for data conversion equipment.

Travel, materials, subcontractors, special equipment, and similar costs associated with a project are classified as miscellaneous expenses. They are collected and put into the system to track actual miscellaneous costs and compare them with estimated miscellaneous costs.

Activity status information reports work progress. It requires an evaluation of the quantity and quality of work performed since the preceding reporting period. The analysis and evaluation should be performed with candor and honesty. Status reporting is the basis for comparing the actual work schedule with the projected schedule. Erroneous reporting of activity status destroys the project control system. Management should review reported activity status to verify the accuracy of reporting.

SUMMARY

The four key documents that can be produced during the initiative phase of a project are the user request, user proposal, feasibility study, and project plan.

The user request is prepared by the user and describes a desired service, and a systems analyst prepares a user proposal to satisfy the user request. The latter contains:

A brief description of the project
User responsibilities
A final date for proposal acceptance
Major project tasks
Estimated developmental costs by task
Annual system operating costs
Project organization and staffing

If the analyst interview with the user indicates that the request requires substantial investigation, a feasibility study may be recommended. The feasibility study is intended to determine whether the time and cost required to develop a data system can be justified. The resources required to conduct an adequate feasibility study are often underestimated. The following are some basic rules:

- Top management should review and support the study.
- The purpose of the study and methodology should be stated to affected employees.
- The study should recognize that some systems should not be automated.
- Alternative designs should be given a real evaluation.
- The statement of conclusions and recommendations should contain a description of the present and proposed system, the resources required to develop the proposed system, and the benefits of the proposed system. The study should also contain a tentative time schedule for decisions and activities.

After the user authorizes a project, a detailed project plan should be prepared. The project plan subdivides the work to be accomplished into subunits or modules and establishes control points. Bar charts or CPM/PERT networks can be used to plan and schedule work tasks. The project manager is responsible for quantitative control, which requires comparing budgeted with actual manpower, machine, and cost expenditures, and qualitative control, which requires review of work for completeness and overall quality.

In addition to bar chart or CPM/PERT outputs, typical reports that are produced to control a project are a project activity report, production by employee report, summary project progress report, and an employee production by work code report.

4. Analysis

The documents outlined in this chapter are user-oriented. Policy and middle management require these documents to understand, in their terms, the system to be developed and their responsibilities for system operation and maintenance. The data processing manager is provided with guidelines for documenting user needs and requirements.

During the analysis phase of a project, the old system, if there is one, is studied and a functional description of the new system, showing utilization of the old, is prepared. A data requirements document defining data elements and specifying data collection requirements will also be prepared if a substantial user effort is required to generate input data and maintain files.

FUNCTIONAL DESCRIPTION (FD)

A *functional description provides the user with a clear statement of the operational capabilities of the data system to be developed.*

If the scope of the functional description is changed at any point during system development, the description should be updated and the changes approved by the user.

The functional description is a technical document written in user language because many elements of the document will be subject to review by personnel who do not have a computer background. *It should be reviewed and formally approved by the user prior to detailed system development.* The document is intended to obtain user concurrence on the capabilities of the data system to be developed and to freeze changes to system specifications. The functional description will have the following content:

1. Objectives and background
   - Purpose of the description
   - Project references
2. System overview
   - Project background
   - Data system objectives
   - Existing methods and procedures
   - Proposed methods and procedures
   - Assumptions and constraints
3. Detailed specifications
   - Performance requirements
   - Data system functions
   - Inputs/outputs descriptions
   - File descriptions
   - System backup and recovery
4. Operating environment
   - Equipment environment
   - Software environment
   - System interfaces
   - Security requirements
5. Cost considerations
   - Developmental costs
   - Operating costs

6. Developmental plan
   Responsibility assignments
   Time schedule

To prepare this document, the analysts refine system descriptions contained in the user proposal and feasibility study. For example, the basic system may be subdivided into functional subsystems. The information flow through each subsystem and the relations between subsystems and system are described. The relations define the files and the boundaries of each subsystem. The impact of the data system on existing methods and procedures also is discussed.

The objective of the functional description is to present the planned data system to the user in clear, unambiguous language that the user can understand. The responsibility of the user is to study the functional description and either approve it or request its modification prior to the start of detailed design work.

Some of the common deficiencies that can limit the usefulness of a functional description are the following:

User involvement in the preparation of the specifications has been inadequate.

The system specifications are shallow and too general.

The old system has not been studied in enough depth.

User approval of the specifications was not obtained prior to detailed design work.

The proposed data system is too complex for the user personnel and user environment.

The developmental time schedule is unrealistic.

If the preparation of a functional description is bypassed during system development, user changes during the design and development phases will usually delay or destroy the project. The proper time for users to change data system specifications is during review of the functional description, when the impact of the changes should be minimal. Specification changes later in the data system development cycle are usually extremely disruptive, costly, and demoralizing.

The user must be directly involved in the preparation of the functional description. One of the common deficiencies in the document is that user requirements are poorly defined. The analyst may have spent insufficient time interviewing user personnel to understand their needs and objectives. System specifications based on insufficient data gathering from users will be shallow and probably inaccurate.

Skill in interviewing is very important during the preparation of the functional description. Data gathering by means of interviews is the primary method of collecting data to define user requirements. The systems analyst must be able to prepare interview questions and questionnaires, establish rapport with interviewees, conduct interviews, and document the information obtained. He can win user cooperation and support for the data system to be developed by involving the user in the definition of specifications for the new system.

In addition to interviewing users, the systems analyst must study the existing system and its methods and procedures in sufficient depth. The new data system will replace an existing system, and therefore the functions to be assumed by the new system must be clearly defined. If the new system fails to assume necessary functions that had been performed by the old system, it may be impossible or difficult to implement. In general, analysts preparing functional descriptions tend not to spend enough time studying existing methods and procedures.

The new system functions may simply be ill-defined. The systems development staff working with the ill-defined system functions may then make invalid assumptions or misinterpretations that will seriously impede the data systems project. Therefore, the analyst preparing the functional description must seek to write clear, precise definitions of the functions to be performed by the data system.

Users of data processing often move too rapidly into complex technical and operational environments. The result is user personnel disorientation and operating problems. If a manual or batch system can be phased in steps into a complex on-line environment with new methods and procedures, the probability of the new data system being successfully implemented is increased. The user personnel have time to adjust mentally to the new system and learn the new procedures.

Another common deficiency in functional descriptions is an unrealistic developmental time schedule. The chronic problem in the data processing industry of developmental project time and cost overruns is often reflected in the unrealistic schedules contained in functional descriptions. The result is that, right from the start, the data system project is in trouble from a time schedule and cost viewpoint. Inexperienced data processing personnel commonly underestimate the time, people, money, and other resources necessary to implement a data system.

Some of the factors that should be considered by the analyst preparing the project time schedule are:

Unusually difficult conversion requirements.
Extensive user personnel training requirements.
Poor cooperation from key departments or personnel.
Need for the preparation of extensive clerical instructions.
Vague user definition of requirements resulting in extensive analysis and design work.
Expected personnel turnover on the developmental project team.
Constraints on the availability of machine time and similar resources for system testing and implementation.

OBJECTIVES AND BACKGROUND

The functional description is in a sense a contract between the user and the system developers that defines the capabilities of the data system that will be developed and delivered to the user. The objectives of the functional description should be set forth in the following way:

> *This Functional Description for [project name and number] is written to describe:*
>
> - *The data system capabilities to be developed that will serve as the basis for an agreement between the user and the developmental staff.*
> - *The impact of the data system on existing methods and procedures.*

- *The performance requirements, system functions, and input/output requirements of the data system.*
- *The hardware/software environment in which the system will operate.*

A summary of references to provide background history of the project should be included. The nature of the computer programs to be developed (payroll, sales analysis, inventory) should be specified. The project sponsor, user, and the data center that will run the operational computer programs should also be indicated. The following documents, if they are available, are referenced or included:

User Request (UR)
User Proposal (UP)
Feasibility Study (FS)
Project Plan (PP)
Other Technical Documentation
Significant Correspondence
Relevant Technical Manuals

SYSTEM OVERVIEW

The system overview section of the functional description describes the proposed data system in user-oriented, nontechnical language. The background and objectives of the system are reviewed to familiarize the reader with the project. If appropriate, reference is made to the existing system and other data systems that are related to the one being developed.

The major performance goals or objectives of the system are concisely and clearly stated. If appropriate, examples are included to clarify the requirements. Typical goals are:

The automation of a manually functioning system
Improved reporting to middle and policy management
Improved user access to information and data files
Faster response to user information inquiries
Better user or customer service

Key management decisions necessary for the successful development of the data system are discussed, and so are planned operational changes that will affect the data system.

The system overview section should describe existing methods and procedures. The following information about existing methods and procedures should be provided:

Organizational structure
Personnel assignments
Equipment being utilized
System inputs and outputs
Existing information files
Work volumes and frequencies
Work flow
Cost of operation
System deficiencies

The existing system, if appropriate, should be described with organization and system flow charts. The system flow charts should illustrate the flow of data through the existing system. They should depict data input, processing, and output. The decision-making functions supported by the existing system should be described.

Next the proposed data system and its capabilities should be briefly discussed. Figure 4-1 shows the information flow in a data system. As shown in Figure 4-2, which illustrates a payroll data system, system flow charts should be employed to depict the general information flow of the system. The charts indicate the major steps necessary to process source data and produce meaningful output information. Interactions with other systems and organizations should be indicated in the organization and system flow charts.

The specific benefits to be derived from the new system should be stated. Some that might be possible are:

Elimination of an inefficient existing function or system
Improved transaction processing time

Figure 4-1. Data system structure.

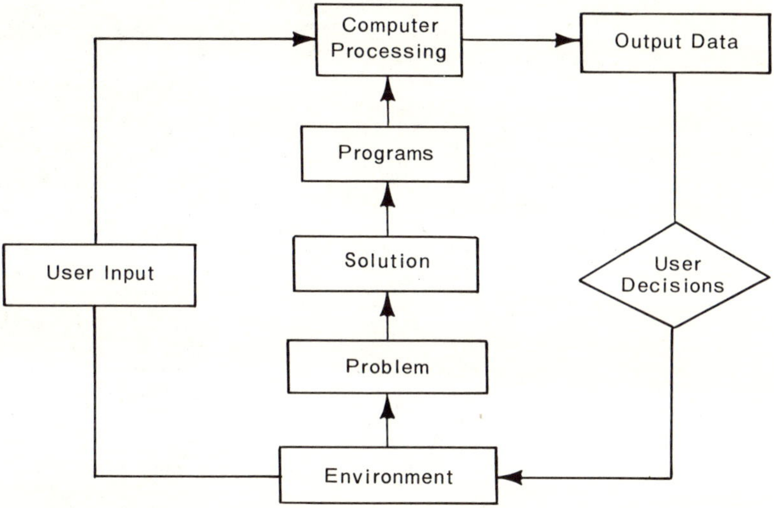

The establishment of new processing or reporting capabilities
Improved inquiry response time
Cost reduction

The impact of the new system on existing methods and procedures should be described. A new data system can have impact on users, organization structures, operating environments, and equipment and software.

User responsibilities to develop, parallel run, implement, and operate the data system should be described. The discussion should include policy decisions and manpower, machine, and money commitments necessary to convert to and then operate the system. The user responsibilities to convert existing files and test the new system prior to live operation should be clearly defined.

The new system may require such organizational changes as the creation of new job positions, the reassignment of personnel, or modified reporting relations. The impact of the new system on personnel

Figure 4-2. Payroll processing flow chart.

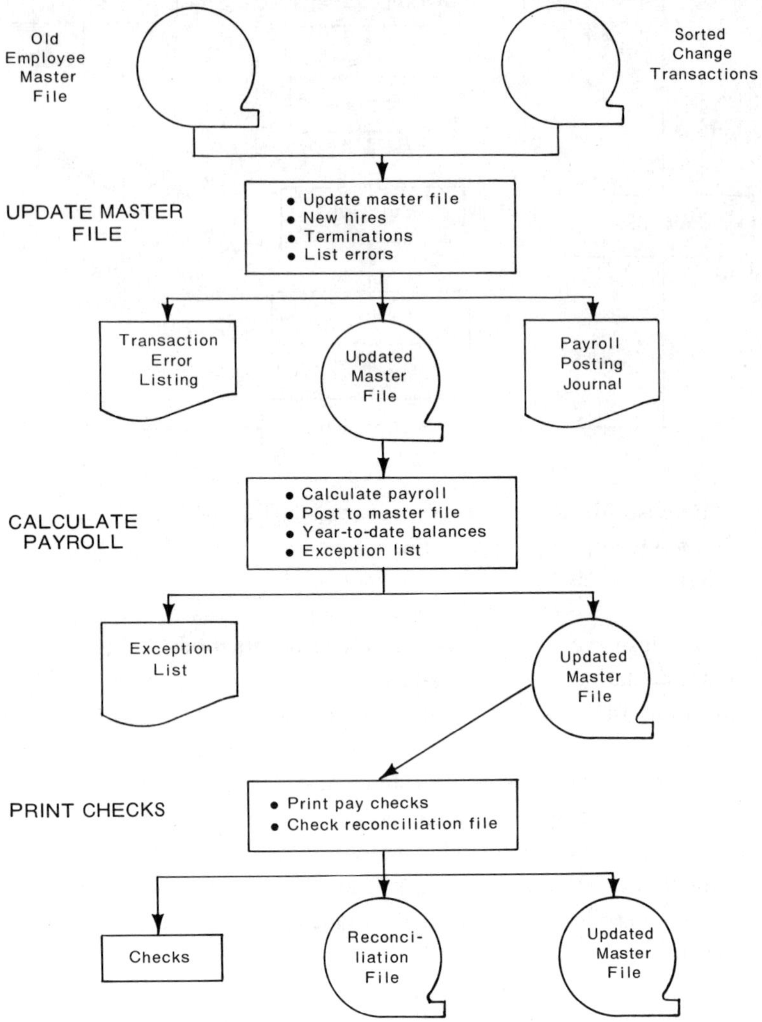

staffing levels and skill categories should be specifically indicated. Both user and data processing personnel training or retraining requirements should be specified.

A new data system can have many impacts on an established data center operating environment. Those impacts should be described. Some of the new requirements the system may impose on the environment are a need for:

Additional computer processing time
Additional file storage space
Additional data conversion personnel
Additional computer operators
New security procedures
New fallback and backup procedures
New data center operating procedures
New data center–user relations

Both the positive and negative effects of the new system on the existing operating environment should be identified.

New equipment and software requirements should be discussed. The equipment requirements can range from the addition to or removal of equipment from an existing installation to the installation of a complete new computer system. Software requirements can include modifications to existing application programs, job control language changes, reprogramming, and operating system changes or conversions. Simulations of the data system should be described, especially as they affect the systems operational capabilities. All assumptions made by the system developers should also be stated.

DETAILED SPECIFICATIONS

The detailed specifications section describes system performance requirements, functions, inputs/outputs, data structures, and system backup requirements.

Specific system performance requirements describe such constraints as the following:

Job throughput time
Terminal response time
Job priority levels
System reliability requirements
System expansion capability
Teleprocessing capabilities
Security and privacy requirements

The system functions described will relate to the specific application being automated. The functions described should be related, when appropriate, to the system performance requirements. In a payroll system the functions to be automated that should be described in detail include:

Edit payroll source data
Calculate earnings and deductions
Update year-to-date balances
Produce payroll checks and earnings statements
Produce a labor distribution and departmental summary
Produce a bond status report
Produce 941A and W-2 statements
Accumulate control totals

The inputs and outputs to the data system should be described. As shown in Figure 4-3, the data inputs are identified by name, record size, volume, medium, and frequency. The output reports are identified by name, frequency, and volume. On-line terminal data inputs and outputs are also described by name, volume, medium, and frequency. The description of data inputs and outputs should include descriptions of editing and quality control requirements. If possible, layouts of terminal screen displays, input records, and output reports should be included.

The description of data structures will include an identification of data elements and files to be utilized by the data system. As shown in Figure 4-4, each file is identified by name, size, medium, and update frequency. If possible, specific data elements, as well as relevant tables and reference files, should be described. The total file storage require-

Figure 4-3. Input/output descriptions.

Name	Input				Frequency
	# Records	Record Size (Bytes)	Volume (Bytes/Mo)	Medium	

Report Name	# Copies	# Parts	# Pages	Lines/Page	Frequency

ments of the system, including on-line and off-line files, should be calculated to match the system storage requirements to equipment storage capabilities. The calculation should include provision for expected file growth.

Figure 4-4. File description form.

File Label	File Name	Medium	System/Subsystem	File Organization	Date

Item No.	Record Name	Record Size (Bytes)	Number of Records	Total Bytes	Update Frequency

The backup requirements of the system are usually based on the need to operate after a minor or major equipment or software failure. The possibilities include a manual backup system, the duplication of equipment, degraded operation capabilities, bypass techniques, and backup data centers. The need for backup usually requires the establishment and maintenance of backup files to recover from a major disaster that destroys the original files. System backup usually involves people, files, programs, software, and equipment. System restart procedures after a minor or major failure should also be described.

OPERATING ENVIRONMENT

The operating environment section should describe the environment in which the system will operate, including equipment, facilities, software, security, and interfaces. The description of equipment should specify available equipment and additional equipment required to test and operate the data system. Figure 4-5 shows the basic components of a computer equipment configuration. The equipment requirements should describe:

Central processing units
Primary memory
Input devices
Output devices
Secondary storage
Communications controllers
Terminals

Facilities required to install the equipment should be described.

The description of software should identify the operating system, data management system, programming languages, communications routines, utilities, and similar software required to develop and operate the data system. Each software system should be accurately identified by name and version number. Software reference manuals, when appropriate, should be specified.

The interfaces of the data system with other systems should be indi-

Figure 4-5. Basic computer configuration components.

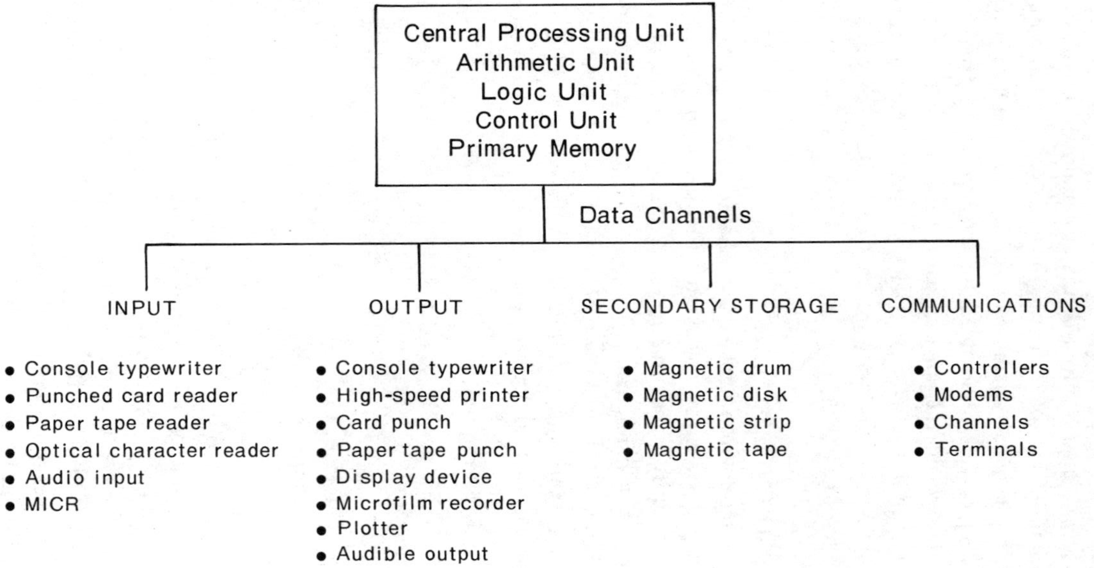

cated. The following information should be supplied for each interface:

Nature of the interface
Data transfer requirements
Formats and protocols
Responsibilities
Frequency of transfer
Data volumes
Editing and checking requirements
Security requirements

Confidential and classified information to be processed by the data system, including programs, files, and documents, should be identified. Procedures to handle this information should be indicated. A typical security program will include rules for:

General administration
Procedural security
Personnel practices
Systems development controls
Computer operation
Physical site security
System reliability

Security is concerned with the protection of information from modification, unauthorized disclosure, willful destruction, misuse, and natural disaster. Security requires that we protect information files and related equipment and software from a variety of man-related threats and natural hazards. *Security measures will involve persons, software, and equipment.*

Individuals can either intentionally or unintentionally physically abuse or mishandle equipment and/or information files and thereby destroy or damage equipment, files, and programs. Another human threat is the individual who obtains access to information that he then modifies or uses without authorization. Many cases can be cited in which data center personnel have defrauded governmental organizations, banks, insurance companies, and brokerage houses. The integrity problem related to the internal data processing staff of managers, analysts, programmers, and operators can be reduced by means of improved hiring policies, background and security checks, the separation of duties, rotating work shifts, and controlling access to sensitive information.

Well-documented and enforced procedures and standards will reduce the probability of a human error that disrupts processing or destroys information. Such controls as file identity checks, checkpoint restart, record counts, sequence checks, and proper operator training should minimize the occurrence of human errors.

The external problem involves users, competitors, criminals, contractors, and "friends" of data center employees. A combination of physical site, software, and procedural security measures combined with improved internal data center hiring and personnel policies will reduce the external threat. An external threat could involve an individual who either by himself or with coconspirators inside the data center seeks to penetrate safeguards and obtain sensitive or valuable information.

The software problem involves user programs, the computer operating system (OS), and data management system (DMS) software. A plot to defraud or embezzle money from an organization may include the modification of computer programs. Master copies of programs can be utilized to audit specific programs periodically and verify that they have not been changed without authorization. Test transactions can also be used to check the validity of operational computer programs. Organizations should plan to check and validate programs randomly to counter the threat to security. In addition, access to libraries containing operational programs should be restricted to authorized personnel.

The computer staff defines rules and procedures to control file creation, updating, and retrieval. They also control user access to information files. They should check user identification numbers or keys for validity, maintain a master profile or description of each user, and determine the specific files to which each user can have access. Each user can be authorized to have access to specific files, and the software will match user profiles to file classifications. The software safeguard will minimize the possibility of a user accidentally having access to a sensitive information file.

The hardware problem involves the protection of equipment and facilities from intentional or accidental damage or destruction. An increasing number of data centers are operating complex data networks with many remote user terminals. A typical network will consist of terminals, data sets, communications lines, concentrators, communications computers, main computer systems, and file storage devices.

Security of a computer network includes consideration of the types of terminal identification keys to be utilized, physical security of terminal locations, terminal locking devices, disposal of terminal output, and data scrambling or encryption. Equipment failures, crosstalk, signal radiation, and taps can lead to the unauthorized disclosure of sensitive information.

Disgruntled employees, ex-employees, radicals, pranksters, dissident groups, and similar persons pose the primary threat of willful equipment destruction or modification. A combination of measures such as improved hiring policies, background checks, controlling access to computer facilities, rotating personnel, utilizing identity badges, documenting emergency procedures, and backup files will reduce the magnitude of the intentional equipment destruction problem.

Accidental damage to equipment and files can be caused by fire, water, wind, and similar natural hazards. Power and air conditioning failures also pose threats that can disrupt the operation of a data center. Safeguards should be developed against fire, flood, windstorm, and similar natural disasters. The security program will require documented disaster procedures and the creation of off-site backup files and programs to permit recovery after a major natural disaster.

COST CONSIDERATIONS

The cost considerations section should review the data system developmental and operating costs. The costs should be compatible with those contained in the user proposal and project plan. Factors or considerations that could change the costs should be identified. Alternative approaches to the design, development, or implementation of the data system that could influence developmental or operating costs should be presented.

DEVELOPMENTAL PLAN

Management decisions that are necessary to successful system design and development should be identified. User responsibilities for the successful development of the data system should be clearly described. The developmental plan should be stated in terms of time schedules, manpower assignments, and equipment delivery schedules, and it should be compatible with the user proposal and project plan.

DATA REQUIREMENTS DOCUMENT (DR)

The data requirements document simplifies the coordination of standard data elements during the development of a data system. *It is normally prepared when a large data collection effort by the user is required to generate and maintain system files.*

The DR is a user-oriented technical document prepared by both systems and user personnel. It is to be as detailed as possible concerning the definition of inputs required of the user, the procedures to be followed to provide the input to the system, the description of expected output data, the specification of all uses of standard data elements, and the data limitations of the system. *The analysis to produce the data requirements document should include user personnel on the analysis team.* The study must be detailed enough to produce a meaningful definition of data elements and relations.

The names and associated codes of data elements should be standardized to facilitate data exchange and commonality of data structures. The standard data elements and data element codes should be used whenever applicable in all data base files. The document can be subdivided as follows:

1. Objectives and background
    - Purpose of data requirements document
    - Project references
2. Data description
    - Static system data
    - Dynamic system data
    - Control and performance data
    - Assumptions and constraints
3. User responsibilities
    - User procedures
    - Editing and conversion requirements
    - Data element descriptions
    - Output report descriptions
    - Impact of data system

OBJECTIVES AND BACKGROUND

The objectives of the data requirements document should be described as follows:

> *This Data Requirements Document for [project name and number] is written to define data elements that the system will process and state user data collection responsibilities.*

There should be a summary of the references applicable to the history of the project. The general nature of the computer programs to be developed is specified. The project sponsor, user, and data center that will operate the completed data system is indicated. The following documents will, if appropriate, be referenced:

User Request (UR)
User Proposal (UP)
Functional Description (FD)
Technical Documents

The scope and magnitude of expected user support for data collection should be stated. The procedure for adding to or modifying the data descriptions that are contained in the document should be specified.

DATA DESCRIPTION

The data described in this section can be classified as relatively constant or static and variable or dynamic.

The static system data consist of tables and reference data utilized by the data system that are infrequently changed. The data elements comprising the static and dynamic data should be identified, listed, and grouped by function:

Alpha and numeric range of values of each element.
Editing and conversion routines performed on each element.
Volume and frequency of each element.
Frequency of element update.
Data system output forms and media of each element.
Expected increase in the byte size and volumes of elements.

Figure 4-6 illustrates a data element description form and Figure 4-7 a record description form. The output reports that will be received by the user organization may also be defined in detail to familiarize user personnel with expected data system outputs. Figure 4-8 shows an output report description form.

The impact of the data elements, records, files, and data base described in the data requirements document on the existing equipment, software, user, and operational environment should be stated. The discussion will further amplify the summary of impacts contained in the functional description.

Assumptions and constraints on the expansion of the system should be stated. For example, the defined data element, record, and file formats and sizes may limit future expansion. Such constraints should be clearly stated.

Figure 4-6. File description form.

Data Element Name	Description	Origin	Size (Bytes)	Type Data	Volume	Frequency
Group Name						
Remarks						

Figure 4-7. Record description form.

Record Name	Origin	Destination	System/File
Size (Bytes)	Media	Volume	Frequency

Item No.	Record Positions	Data Element Name	Label	Size (Bytes)	Type Data	Remarks

Figure 4-8. Output reports.

Report Name	Origin	Destination/User	Media
Number of Copies	Number of Pages	Lines per page	Run Frequency

Item No.	Report Positions	Data Element Name	Label	Size (Bytes)	Type Data	Remarks

USER RESPONSIBILITIES

This section describes user responsibilities for the collection, editing, and processing of the data elements that have been listed. It defines user information necessary for the system developers to determine the values of the system data elements.

The organization(s) responsible for supplying the data elements to the operational data system and their responsibilities during the system development and implementation phases should be described. The procedure to be followed by user personnel in the collection of data elements should be stated. Formats and procedural flow charts should be included. The specific daily, weekly, and monthly time requirements for the user input of data elements to the data system should be indicated. The following user information may be necessary to document the system data elements:

Origin of the data elements specified by organization.
Methods of conversion to machine-readable form.
Input media for entry of data elements into the data system.
Destination of data elements in terms of organizations or computer programs.
Alpha and numeric range of values of each data element.
Editing and conversion routines performed on each data element.
Volume and frequency of each data element.
Frequency of data element update.
Data system output forms and media of each data element.
Expected increase in the byte size and volumes of data elements.

SUMMARY

The primary documents produced during the analysis phase of a project are the functional description and the data requirements document. The functional description is a user-oriented document intended to serve as an agreement between the user and developer as to the capabilities of the planned data system. It should be reviewed and formally approved by the user prior to further system development. The document refines previous system descriptions and describes the information flow through each subsystem and the relation between subsystems. It should be written in clear, unambiguous language that can be understood by the user.

Skill in interviewing simplifies the preparation of this document. The ability of the analyst to develop a data-gathering methodology, establish rapport with interviewees, and obtain meaningful information from interviews is reflected in the quality of the functional description. A document produced after insufficient data gathering will be shallow and will contribute directly to a developmental project time and cost overrun.

Some basic rules to follow in preparing the functional description are the following:

Get the user organization involved in its preparation.
Study the old system and its methods and procedures in depth.
Match the complexity of the data system being developed to the capabilities of the user organization.
Get formal user approval of the functional description before starting detailed design work.
Beware of unrealistic time and cost schedules.

If the preparation of a functional description is bypassed or if it is deficient, user requests for system changes later in the developmental cycle will probably delay or destroy the project. The document is intended to obtain user concurrence on the capabilities of the planned system and to freeze system changes.

The data requirements document is prepared when a major user effort is required to handle input data and maintain system files. It is also a user-oriented document and is intended to provide the user with a clear definition of user responsibilities, data inputs required of the user, and a definition of standard data elements.

The organization(s) responsible for data collection and editing is or are identified. Formats and procedural flow charts are usually included to guide user personnel. The data requirements document defines:

Origin of data elements
Conversion requirements
Data element definitions
Record definitions
Editing requirements
Data volumes and frequencies
Output forms and reports

The impact of the data system on the user environment is described, and this amplifies the functional description.

5.

Design

This chapter provides policy and middle management with guidelines that can be used in the evaluation of the quality and completeness of information system design specifications. It also includes a discussion of the data management software that can be utilized to create, maintain, and provide access to information files. The data processing manager is provided with a review of the structure and content of the key design phase documents.

In the design phase of a project, detailed specifications for the new system are prepared. The detailed design specifications represent a level of detail beyond the functional description. The output from the design phase is a detailed design report that will vary in size with the magnitude of the system being developed. For complex systems, the detailed design specifications may be modularized into system/subsystem specifications, data base specifications, and program specifications.

SYSTEM/SUBSYSTEM SPECIFICATIONS (SS)

A system specification or subsystem specifications may be prepared to guide the development of a large project. If the system breaks down readily into subsystems, the document may be used to prepare individual subsystem definitions. Many systems, however, cannot be broken down into smaller components because they do not have logically distinct modules. In that case, this document outline can be used to write a system specification.

The system/subsystem specifications should represent a level of detail beyond the functional description that supports the system functions, environment, and design requirements. In general, a good functional description simplifies the preparation of good system/subsystem specifications.

The design of a batch data system is usually simpler than that of a real-time, terminal-oriented system. In a real-time system, system response time is of primary importance and shapes the design of the system. Because of the communications hardware and software in a real-time system, there are more variables that can adversely affect system performance. Troubleshooting and problem isolation in a real-time environment can be extremely complex. When a real-time, terminal-oriented system fails, users are immediately aware of the problem and pressure immediately builds to resume operation.

In preparing system/subsystem specifications, the design team should consider the following items:

Sources. The points of origin of the transaction data must be known; the designer must determine both initial and potential locations that will generate transaction data. For example, payroll transaction information may be entered into the central computer system from terminals.

Destinations. The designer must determine the locations that will receive output from the system. For example, a user may query the system for the on-hand balance of an item in inventory. The query will be entered into a remote terminal and processed by the computer at the central facility. The answer will be routed back to the remote terminal.

Data formats. The designer must determine the formats of the information being processed. He must trace information through the complete entry-to-output cycle. The format of the information may vary as it passes through the cycle.

Information volumes. The analyst must determine expected information volumes and define types and numbers of messages. The designer must ascertain the stability of the volumes because there may be significant fluctuation or a steady increase.

Message frequencies. The analyst must establish message frequencies. The message traffic must be broken out by hour, day, and month. The frequency information will determine the system's peak periods. An overload condition will result if the network cannot handle the peak periods.

Response time. The designer must determine system response requirements. System response time is the interval during which a user must wait for an answer to a query. It will directly affect the user's satisfaction with the system. The designer must first establish the required response time and then design and implement a system that can achieve it. In many applications—on-line banking, airline reservation systems, hospital systems—the response time is a key element in customer satisfaction.

Reliability. The design study must establish the system reliability parameters. The consequences of a system malfunction or failure must be investigated. The seriousness of a malfunction or failure will vary with the application being automated.

System balance. The circuits, hardware, software, and terminals that comprise the network should be balanced. For example, it is wasteful to have circuit capacities that far exceed the needs of the terminals or central computer facility. A balance must also be achieved between the hardware and circuits necessary to operate the system and those necessary for backup.

Data editing. Many systems have been developed without adequate ways to identify and flag invalid input data prior to processing. The need for data editing is obvious, but control has often not been adequately stressed in the design of data systems.

Security. Adequate system controls include security procedures, audit trails, and backup procedures. These controls also are often not adequately considered in the design of data systems.

Performance monitoring. System performance controls are related to the accumulation of performance statistics. Too often management does not have enough information for an intelligent review of the efficiency of an operational data system.

Exception reporting. When management reporting is by exception, only exceptional transactions or conditions are flagged for attention. A common policy and middle management complaint is that all possible data are included in reports and that they receive stacks of computer printout rather than only the information they need.

Cost. Cost will usually be a constraint in the design of the system; the system should represent a balance between cost and performance.

If any of the software, hardware, or personnel elements in a system are inadequate or unreliable, the entire system will be degraded. For example, inadequate priority and queuing routines in the operating system software will slow system response time. An inefficient data management system also will affect response time, and limitations in the central processing unit, memory, or peripheral devices will degrade system performance. Improperly trained central site operators or remote terminal personnel will create operational problems. The art of system design requires that the designer build a system that has functionally integrated and efficient components.

The design of a network computer system requires a thorough investigation of the communications requirements of the system. Computer systems depend so heavily on communications that any deficiencies in the computer, terminals, circuits, data sets, multiplexers, and similar equipment can jeopardize the entire network.

System balance means that the components of the system are properly balanced to minimize bottlenecks or bound points. Figure 5-1 illustrates the major hardware components of a computer-based communications network. The elements of the network computer system are the central computer, communications controllers, data sets, communications circuits, concentrators, and remote terminals.

Central computer. Transaction information and user inquiries are fed into the computer for processing from the remote terminals.

Communications controller. The communications controller controls several communications circuits at the same time and manages the receipt and transmission of messages over the communications lines.

Data sets. A data set is a device that converts data to a form suitable for sending and receiving on communications facilities.

Communications facility. The communications facility is a circuit between two points for the purpose of transmitting and receiving information. Some examples of communications facilities are telegraph cables, telephone cables, and microwave channels.

Narrow-band facility. A narrow-band facility is one that is unable to transmit voice but can transmit slower-speed data. Transmission is at telegraph speed, under 200 bits per second. Narrow-band facilities offer the lowest data transmission capability.

Voice-band facility. A voice-band facility is one that can be used for either voice or data transmission. It is a circuit with a sufficient bandwidth to permit a transfer rate of up to 2,400 bits per second. The

Figure 5-1. Representative communications network.

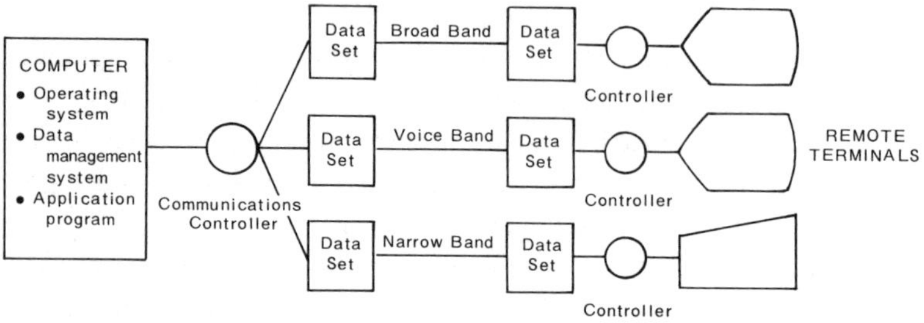

public telephone network employs voice-band circuits. This type of service is commonly used for computer networks.

Broad-band facility. A broad-band facility is one that is able to simultaneously carry many voice or data circuits. This service is capable of high-speed data communications at speeds up to several million bits per second. The broad-band channel can be subdivided to provide several independent channels of lower capacity. Broad-band service has the highest data transfer capacity. It is utilized when large volumes of data must be transmitted between two points.

Concentrators. A network might utilize communications concentrators. A communications concentrator—usually a small computer—serves as a switch for the terminals in a geographic area. The central computer is linked by a communications circuit to the concentrator. The concentrator is linked, in turn, by circuits to the terminals. Data are received by the concentrator from the terminals and directed to the central computer. Information is received by the concentrator from the central computer and directed to the appropriate terminal.

Terminals. The terminals on the network may vary greatly. They will be oriented in capability to the user's application. A network may have many different types of terminals. A terminal may range from a very simple keyboard query station to a complex subsystem having high-speed printers, card read/punch capability, keyboards, and a visual display. The type of terminal depends upon the scope of tasks to be performed.

Interactive terminals. Interactive terminals permit an active dialogue between the terminal user and the central computer and are required for time-sharing service. Teletypewriters, typewriters, and cathode-ray tubes (CRT's) with keyboards have been most commonly employed. The users might be engineers seeking the solutions to complex algorithms, airline reservation clerks seeking flight availability information, or operating managers checking the on-hand balance of an inventory item.

Remote batch terminals. Remote batch terminals are designed for the input of volume transactions or jobs from a remote terminal. The word "batch" indicates that items are coded and collected into groups before processing. In general, batch terminals are designed for larger volumes of input-output information than interactive terminals can handle. Some batch terminals permit both batch and interactive processing.

Data collection terminals. Data collection terminals are input stations that can be placed in departments or cost centers to capture transaction information. They can record labor, machine, and material charges as they occur. The terminal can record the status of a job, personnel assignments, or the load capacity of a center. The transaction information captured by the data collection terminal in an industrial environment can be utilized to generate the following typical reports:

Efficiency
Job status
Man/machine load
Machine downtime
Labor distribution
Material shortage
Updated inventory
Scrap and rework control
Daily issues and receipts
Tool availability and charge-out

Some of the typical bottlenecks in computer systems to be avoided are inefficiencies or limitations caused by:

Application program software
Operating system software
Data management system software
Poorly trained operators
Inadequately trained users
Poor data base design
Excessive disk head movements
Inadequate central processing unit power

Primary memory limitations
Data channel imbalance
Poorly designed communications network
Inadequate communications controller

Future teleprocessing systems will be affected by a predicted increase in the use of:

Intelligent terminals
Applications-oriented terminals
Distributed data bases
Specialized communications computers
Duplexed main computer systems
Virtual memories
Data management software

The system/subsystem specification has the following content:

1. Objectives and background
    - Purpose of system/subsystem specification
    - Project references
2. System overview
    - System/subsystem requirements
    - System/subsystem functions
    - Assumptions and constraints
3. Operating environment
    - Equipment environment
    - Software environment
    - System interfaces
    - Security requirements
    - Control requirements
4. Detailed specifications
    - System flow charts
    - Program descriptions
        - Inputs, outputs, and files
    - System backup and recovery

5. Developmental plan
   Responsibility assignment
   Time schedule

OBJECTIVES AND BACKGROUND

The objectives of the system/subsystem specification (SS) should be described as follows:

> *This System/Subsystem Specification for [project name and number] is written to provide:*
> - *A detailed definition of the system/subsystem capabilities to be developed.*
> - *A detailed description of the environment in which the data system will operate.*
> - *Detailed system logical flow and program descriptions.*
> - *A definition of required interfaces with other systems and subsystems.*

References applicable to the history and development of the project should be cited. The project sponsor and user and the data center that will run the completed computer programs should be indicated. The following documents, if they are available, would usually be referenced:

Functional Description (FD)
Data Requirements Document (DR)
Related System/Subsystem Specifications (SS)
Data Base Specifications (DS)
Program Specifications (PS)

SYSTEM OVERVIEW

The system/subsystem specification summarizes the performance requirements and functions of the data system. It expands upon and adds detail to the system requirements stated in the functional description. Changes to the requirements contained in the functional description should be clearly identified.

The characteristics of the system should be summarized to provide the reader with an overview of the data system. Organization and system flow charts should be included to illustrate the system's organizational and data structures. The summary should closely correspond in content with the functional description. The specific requirements or functions of the data system should be described in summary form, and the description should be related to the statement of system requirements contained in the functional description.

As stated in the functional description, specific performance requirements include:

Job throughput time
Terminal response time
Job priority levels
System reliability requirements
System expansion capability
Security requirements

The capability of the data system to incorporate changes such as workload increases, new system interfaces, and additional terminals should be stated. The system's flexibility and modularity should be described. A procedure to make changes to the system, and also all assumptions and constraints that could affect system development or operation, should be identified.

OPERATING ENVIRONMENT

This section of the system/subsystem specifications describes the equipment, software, interfaces, security, and controls necessary to support the data system.

The equipment description should specify the configuration necessary to develop, test, and operate the data system; it should be a more detailed presentation of the equipment requirements outlined in the functional description. Figure 5-2 shows the schematic of a represen-

Figure 5-2. Schematic system diagram.

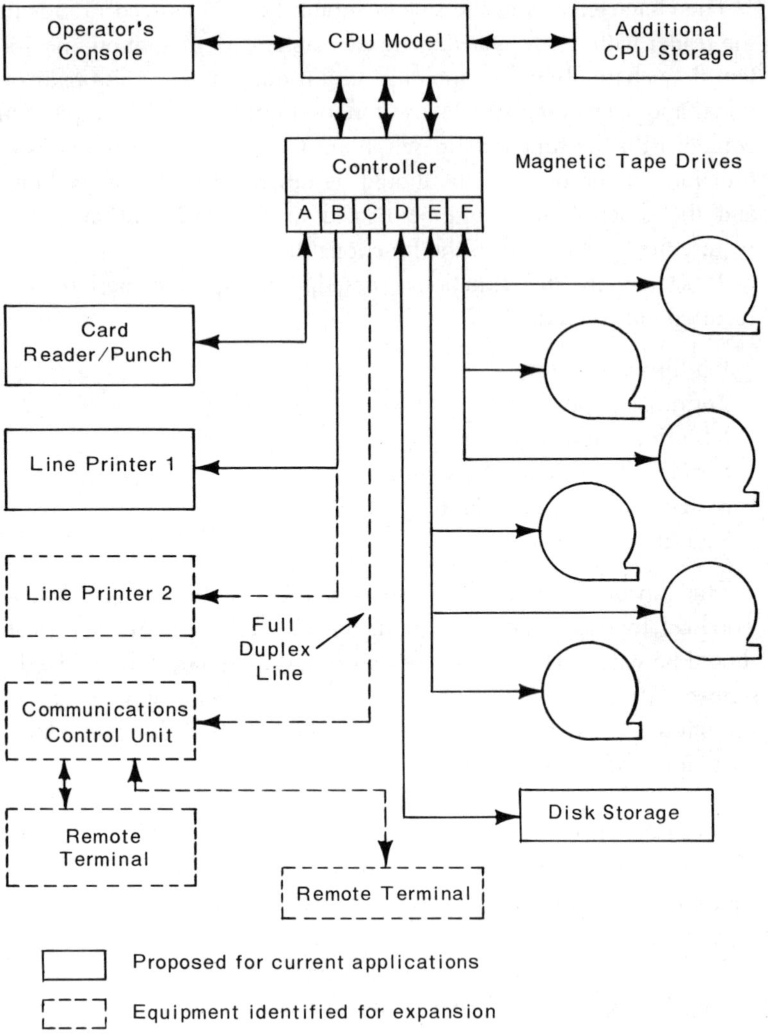

tative computer system. Both the present and planned equipment environments should be defined.

If a new computer system is to be installed, the following equipment should be identified by manufacturer and model number:

Central processing unit
- Primary memory
- Data channels
- Special features

Secondary storage
- Magnetic drum
- Magnetic disk
- Magnetic strip
- Magnetic tape

Input devices
- Console typewriter
- Punched card reader
- Paper tape reader
- Optical character reader (OCR)
- Audio input
- Magnetic ink character reader (MICR)
- Tape cassettes

Output devices
- Console typewriter
- High-speed printer
- Card punch
- Paper tape punch
- Display device
- Microfilm recorder
- Plotter
- Audible output

Communication and terminals
- Communication controller
- Data sets

Communications circuits
Concentrator
Terminals

The software environment description identifies the operating system, data management system, programming languages, communications routines, utilities, and similar software required to develop, test, and operate the data system. Each software system should be identified by name and version number. The description should also expand upon information contained in the functional description. The following software should be described:

Operating system
Data management system
Communications software
Assemblers and compilers: ANSI FORTRAN, ANSI COBOL, PL/1
Utility programs
Sort/merge programs
Diagnostic programs
Report generators
Application packages

The interfaces with other systems and subsystems should be identified. The following requirements stated in the functional description should be confirmed, and additional detail should be supplied:

Nature of the interface
Data transfer requirements
Formats and protocols
Responsibilities
Frequency of transfer
Data volumes
Editing and checking requirements
Security requirements

The following system constraints relating to security, privacy, and confidentiality as stated in the functional description should be confirmed and expanded upon:

General administration
Procedural security
Personnel practices
Systems development control
Computer operation
Physical site security
System reliability

System controls to insure the integrity of the system data should be discussed. Typical controls include:

Limit checks
Arithmetic proof
Identification checks
Label checks
Sequence checks
Record counts
Control totals
Check digits
Special printouts
Audit transactions

DETAILED SPECIFICATIONS

This section describes in detail the logical flow of data in the system and presents all system inputs and outputs. System flow charts, as illustrated in Figure 5-3, are employed to illustrate data flow and the relationship between logic components of the system. As appropriate, narrative descriptions should supplement the system flow charts.

Each computer program comprising the data system should be individually described in detail. The inputs, outputs, and files to be utilized by each program should be presented. Some of the basic data necessary to describe a program include:

Inputs
Title and tag
Sources

Formats
Volume and frequencies
Medium
Editing requirements
Time constraints
Security requirements
Special handling
Means of entry
Priority levels

Outputs

Title and tag
Recipients

Figure 5-3. Payroll check reconciliation system flow.

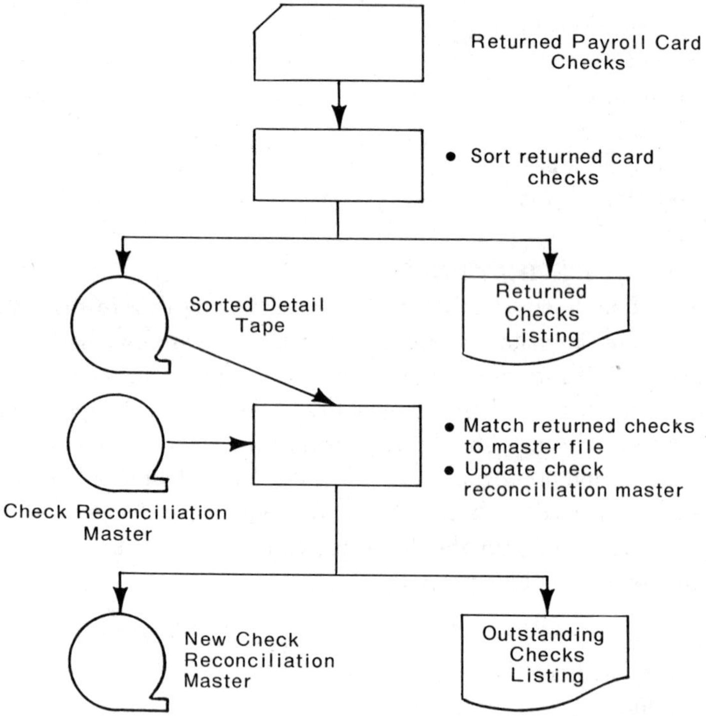

Volume and frequencies
Formats
Medium
Editing requirements
Time constraints
Security requirements
Special handling
Priority levels

Files

Title and tag (file, table, directory)
Description
Number of entries
Format
Medium
Security requirements
Update frequency
Retention cycle

System backup and recovery requirements as defined in the functional description should be restated and, if appropriate, discussed in more detail.

DEVELOPMENTAL PLAN

The organizational and individual responsibilities involved in the successful implementation of the data system should be restated. The time schedule contained in the functional description should, if necessary, be revised. Any effect of development plan changes on data system developmental or operating costs should be stated.

DATA BASE SPECIFICATIONS (DS)

The data base specification describes the system files, tables, and directories. It is a technical document intended to be used by programmers and data base administrators. *It is prepared when the data system being developed has significant file structuring, accessing, and maintenance requirements.*

There is great pressure on data processing managers to develop corporate information systems that support planning, control, and operational functions and provide information fast enough to assist management decision making. Data management systems have been developed to provide frameworks for such corporate information systems.

A *data management system consists of a series of software programs that have the capability to create and update files, select, retrieve, and sort data, and generate reports.* A data management system works with elementary data elements, records, and files. The data elements comprise records that in turn are organized into logic units called files. The arrangement of records in a file forms a data structure that will vary with user processing requirements.

The generally accepted requirements for a system to be known as a data management system include the capability to create, revise, and delete records from a file, an interrogation or information retrieval capability that includes such features as sorting and limited computations, and finally a report-generating capability that can meet user-specified parameters. Additional characteristics may be added to the basic system depending on the capabilities of a specific hardware configuration. Teleprocessing and on-line inquiry capabilities are often added to a data management system.

Major data management systems differ primarily in three areas: language utilized, file organization and access methods, and level of system users.

Language Differences. In the work conducted by the CODASYL Systems Committee, an organization that develops and implements COBOL standards, one of the most important distinctions noted among existing data management systems was the difference between what the committee calls self-contained and host language systems. Self-contained systems usually provide a language designed for the nonprogrammer; host language systems are tied to such languages as COBOL, PL/1, ALGOL, and FORTRAN and are oriented toward the applications programmers who utilize those languages.

Self-contained systems provide their own language, which is user-oriented and designed to be used by managers and others with little or no knowledge of programming. The language is oriented toward data management, and although it employs the style and approach of a procedure-oriented language (POL) such as COBOL, it utilizes formats and verbs specifically developed for data management.

Certain self-contained systems, called forms-controlled systems, differ from others primarily in the form of the language, which is based on checking squares in the boxes on special forms. The forms contain self-explanatory user instructions. Such systems are user-oriented and decrease language errors by decreasing user input. For each box on the form there is a corresponding preprinted instruction to guide the user in completing the form.

Embedded host language systems are basically enhancements of existing languages such as COBOL, FORTRAN, and PL/1. Therefore, they provide all the power of those languages. There are two ways in which the system can be embedded in a host language: by means of a CALL statement in the host language or by adding new statements to the host language.

File Organization and Access Method Differences. A number of different data organization schemes to support data management systems have evolved. User demands differ in response time and output requirements. Consequently, several different file organization techniques and file access methods to support data management systems have evolved.

In examining data management systems, one must separate logical and physical file organization. A study of logical organization will ascertain whether user requirements can be satisfied. A study of physical file organization indicates the handling procedures, file maintenance, retrieval capability, output, and similar operational features of the data management system.

The following outline is suggested for examining file-structuring capabilities.

Logical
- Hierarchical
  - Number of levels
  - Repeating groups
  - Symbolic addresses
- Heterogeneous
  - Number of levels
  - Repeating groups
  - Symbolic addresses
  - Links/pointers

Physical
- Sequential structure
  - Sort fields
- Random structure
  - Computational
  - Lists
- Simple list structure
- Inverted list structure
- Ring structure

The logical file organization is the structure of which the user is aware in designing a file. It may differ from the storage structure, which is the internal machine representation of the data; it is utilized by the user to aggregate the data. Related data elements, the basic entities in the file, are collected into groups, and logically related groups are aggregated into records. The interrelated records are collected to form the logical file format. *The basic structure of the logical file system should be accomplished by the user independently of machine considerations.* In most cases a user does not need to know how or where a file is stored by the data management system.

A *hierarchical structure* provides a master-detail relation that is commonly referred to as the tree structure (see Figure 5-4). A pure hierarchically structured file starts with a single record at the root or base of the structure. From the base the structure can immediately branch out and identify many records that in turn can also branch out. All the records on the same level are peers.

Heterogeneous structures do not have a pure tree-structured hierarchy. Logical linkage is allowed between groups of any level, and a group may be subordinate to one or more superior groups. Links or pointers are required to define the relations of subordinate, peer, and superior. "Network file" is the term commonly used to refer to this kind of logical file structure (see Figure 5–4).

The physical file organization is a function of the data management system and the equipment in which the system operates. It is not necessary that the physical organization of the data reflect the logical organization. It must be pointed out that the following examples are file-structuring concepts, and it is unlikely that a data management system can be restricted to one pure concept.

Physical data organizational methods are built from three basic organizations: sequential, random, and list. In a *sequential organization* records are stored in positions relative to other records in a definite sequence. A common attribute of the records, such as social security number, becomes the key to the ordering sequence.

In a *random organization* records are stored and retrieved on the basis of a predictable relation between the key to the data and the address at which the data are stored. Methods of access in random organization are direct access, index, and calculation. By the direct access method the key to a record can be directly converted to the record address for record retrieval. By the index method a record's key and its direct address can be stored in an index or dictionary that is searched during retrieval. With large files, it may be necessary to divide the indices into levels, the first of which is core resident. Finally, the calculation method is a technique with which a formula can be applied to the record key to compute the record memory address.

A basic concept of the *list organization* is that pointers are used to divorce the logical organization from the physical organization. The main types of list organization are simple list, inverted list, and ring. In a sequential organization the next logical record is also the next

Figure 5-4. Logic structures.

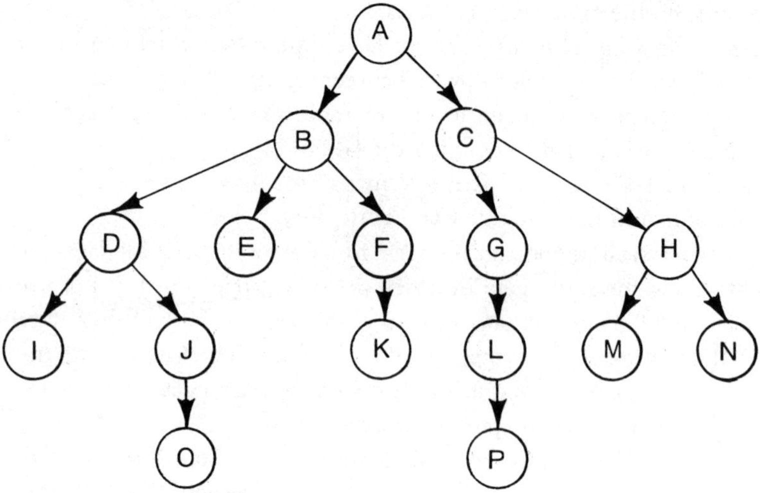

Tree Structure

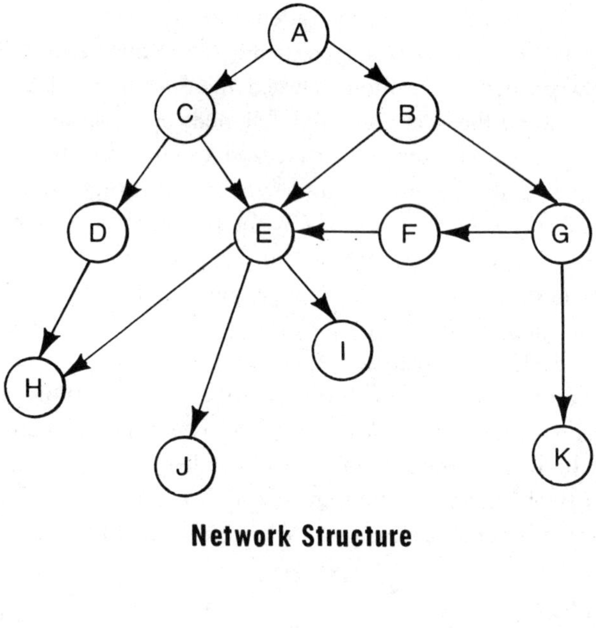

Network Structure

physical record. *In a list structure, by including with each record a pointer or link to the next logical record, the logical and physical organization can be made completely different.* When pointers are included in the records, the result is a chain that may be in the form of a simple list or a circular or ring list. List structures are random-structured; for their pointers are used to divorce the logical and physical organization or introduce multiple logical relations.

A simple list structure (see Figure 5-5) permits any number of keys in a record by associating a pointer with each key. Records with values for specific keys are linked together by the pointers. In an inverted list structure, dictionaries contain each key and the pointer(s) to the records having the same value as the key in the index. No pointers appear in the records containing that particular key value. With an inverted list structure it becomes possible to search, compare, and manipulate the lists of pointers rather than the records to which they point.

In a ring structure, lists are not external to the physical file; they are circular in that the last record in a list points or links to a first record and will not contain an indicator to show that it is the last record in the list. All data elements of a single type are chained together, and each data element on a sublevel is directly linked to its master element. The pointers are used for progression around rings; and by the inclusion of more than one pointer, forward or backward tracing, as well as direct return to the master data element, is possible.

Level of System Users. A data management system makes it possible for various applications to work with a common data base when the data base is an interrelated set of organization files.

Three levels can be defined within the decision-making and data requirement hierarchy. The first, *strategic planning,* is identified with policy management and is applied to determining long-range objectives. *Management control,* the second level, is associated with middle management and the ongoing administration of the organization; it is normally identified with the division head or middle management and

Figure 5-5. List file structures.

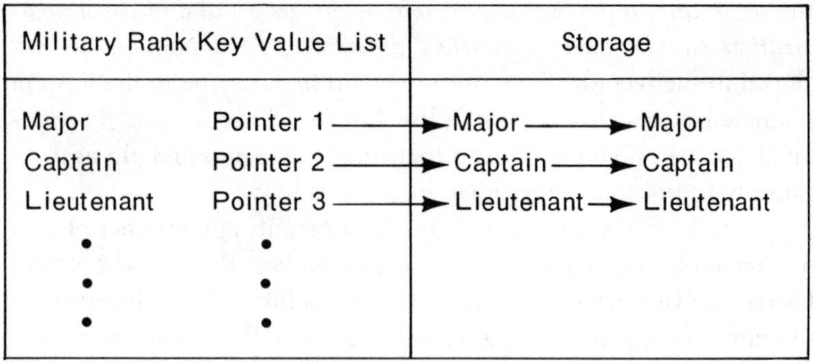

A Simple List Structure

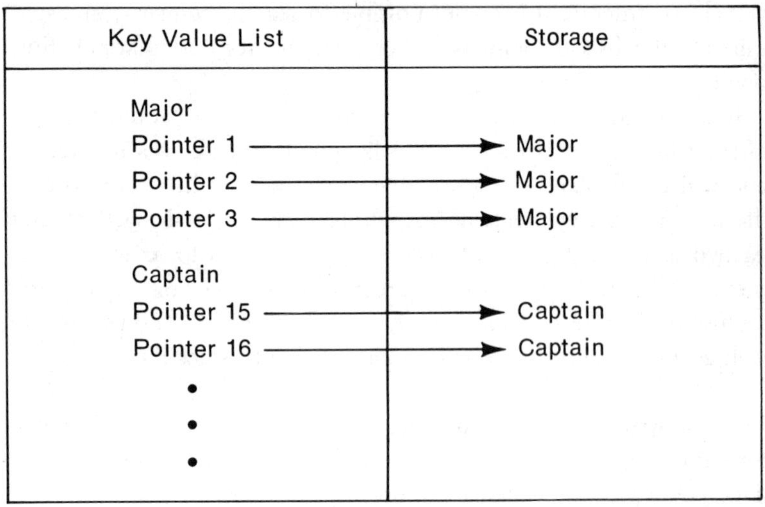

An Inverted List Structure

their efforts to manage the daily operations of a company. The third level is *operational control*, which is normally associated with supervisors and foremen at the working level and is concerned with task performance.

Data requirements differ with the level of user. Policy management will usually require summary reports in contrast to the greater detail required by middle management. The report format requested will vary with the user's level in the organization.

In another user classification, four levels of data management system users are identified: the data base manager, applications programmer, specializer, and general user. The data base manager initially sets up the data base and makes the decisions on data structure to meet his own and other users' needs. The applications programmer is responsible for writing programs to operate on the data base. The specializer understands how to express inquiries or update the data base in the user-oriented language. He may be a manager or lower-level employee. The general user needs no knowledge of programming, nor need he understand the self-contained system language. Examples of this kind of user are bank tellers and retail sales personnel.

As is evident, there are different levels of users with differing demands for information. Each user must be able to address a common data base and receive correct information in the proper format.

The following basic elements can be identified as potential components of a data management system:

- Data base management languages
  - Data definition language
  - Data manipulation language
- Retrieval subsystem
  - Search routines
  - Extract routines
- Processing subsystem
  - Data validation
  - Logic and arithmetic ability
  - Update ability
- Output subsystem
  - Sort-merge
  - Report preparation

Communications subsystem
  Terminal and line-handling capabilities
  Resource allocation
Other elements
  Data security
  Restart and recovery

The Conference on Data Systems Languages (CODASYL) was founded in 1959 to investigate higher-level programming languages for business applications. In April 1960 a manual containing the specifications for a Common Business Oriented Language (COBOL) were issued.

The CODASYL Data Base Task Group (DBTG), in an April 1971 report, presented a proposal that included the specifications for data definition and data manipulation languages to extend COBOL's capability to work with data bases. *The data management language would be a host-language-embedded system with COBOL one of the host languages.* Figure 5–6 illustrates the structure of the proposed system. The issue of whether the DBTG proposal should be accepted as a common industry guide to the structure of future data management systems is now being debated.

Figure 5-6. Structure of 1971 DBTG proposal.

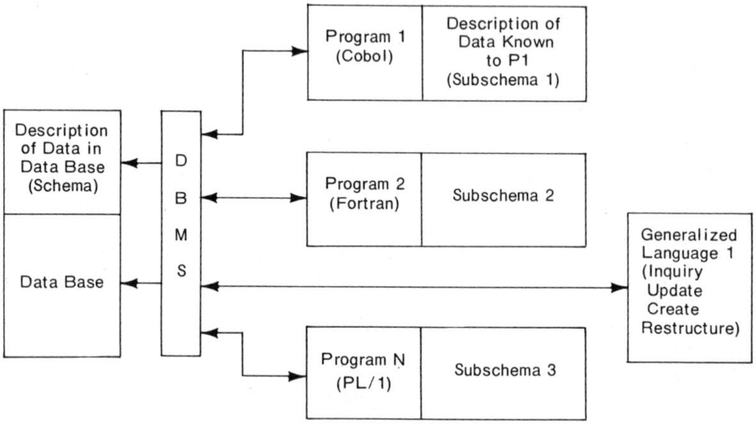

A data description language named the schema DDL was described for defining the complete data base that would be independent of any programming language. This language would be utilized to define records, sets of records, and areas of the universal data base. A COBOL data descriptive language named the COBOL subschema DDL for interfacing COBOL programs with the complete data base was also described in the April 1971 report. A subschema DDL is required for each separate host language application program interfacing with the complete data base.

The word "schema" is employed to identify the part of the data description language that defines the data base itself as opposed to subschema. A subschema is that part of a data description language (DDL) that describes the data known to a given application program written in a host language. There may be many subschema. Usually, the subschema will be less extensive than the schema, since the entire data base may not be needed by a given application.

A COBOL data-manipulative language (COBOL DML) was described for specifying the storage and retrieval actions desired by an application program. The DML relies on a host language to provide a framework for it and also to provide the procedural capabilities to manipulate data. The DML controls the data base and interfaces it, by means of the schema and subschema DDL, to the host language utilized. A user application program would be a mixture of host language and DML statements.

A data management system can be a great benefit to an organization that can utilize its capabilities. The system can significantly reduce the time and cost required to develop a computer-based information system. It can also reduce the time required to satisfy top management information requests.

The user can minimize the time required for file organization, input-output processing, and device type considerations. Programmers can work on difficult programs rather than on the generation of simple reports and file maintenance, and fewer lines of coding will be required to produce programs. A debugged data management system can eliminate the need to test and debug an in-house-developed file management system. Users with little or no prior programming experience can make information queries by utilizing the data management system; and with one system interrogation, a user can extract several different reports in varying formats.

There are also disadvantages of data management systems: the systems can be costly to develop in-house, rent, or purchase. Purchase and rental costs vary substantially, but some systems cost over $100,000. In addition, generalized systems can be relatively inefficient. Just as higher-level languages such as COBOL are considered more inefficient than assembly languages, so data management systems are more inefficient from a machine point of view than higher-level languages.

Another consideration is that these systems are usually machine-dependent. Few systems can operate effectively on more than one type of computer equipment. An organization considering a change to a new hardware system should consider whether the data management system can be transferred to the new system. The potential user should be especially wary of a system that has few users. Such a system may not be fully debugged, and its operational abilities may fall far short of the vendor's claims.

The data base specification format will vary with the specific data base structure utilized by the system designers, and therefore the document must be flexible in both format and method of presentation. The following outline should serve as a guide rather than a rigid framework:

1. Objectives and background
    - Purpose of the data base specification
    - Project references
2. Data base definition
    - Data base labeling conventions
    - Logical file organization
    - Physical file organization
    - Data systems supported
    - Support programs

3. Data descriptions
    - System files
    - Control tables
    - Data elements
    - Data records
4. Storage requirements
    - Primary storage
    - Secondary storage
    - Storage maps
5. Interface requirements
    - Data bases
    - Shared data

OBJECTIVES AND BACKGROUND

The objectives of the data base specification should be described as follows:

> *This Data Base Specification for [project name and number] is written to describe:*
>
> - *The data base structure and its contents.*
> - *The files, tables, and data elements and the records that comprise the data base.*
> - *Methods of accessing and maintaining the data base.*
> - *Data base storage requirements.*
> - *Interface requirements.*

The project sponsor and user and the data center that will run the data system are identified. The following documents, when applicable, should be referenced in the data base specification:

Functional Description (FD)
Data Requirements Document (DR)
System/Subsystem Specifications (SS)
Program Specifications (PS)
Other technical documentation
Technical manuals

DATA BASE DEFINITION

This section describes in detail the organization and physical structure of the data base. The data systems utilizing the data base are identified. The data management software supporting the data base is also discussed.

Unique tags or labels that identify the data base or its files are defined. The relation between this data base and other data bases is stated, and all data systems that will utilize the data base are identified. Effective dates are set to establish the time period during which the data base can be utilized. The physical media on which the data base files will reside should be defined, and relevant characteristics of the media should be discussed. Conventions followed by the designer in assigning tags and labels are stated.

The organization or architecture of the data base and related access and manipulation methods should be described in detail. The information will typically include:

Logical file organization
- Association capabilities
- Flexibility
- Dictionary techniques

Physical file organization
- File load requirements
- Access techniques
- Data space management
- Compression techniques
- Index and file expansion
- Impact of reorganization
- Multiuser capabilities

Valid data formats, machine run instructions, and general rules and procedures to be followed by users to generate and utilize the data base should be described. The programs that support the data base should be identified and described. The operating procedures for these programs, as well as the functions performed by the programs, should be discussed. Typical support programs include:

Data base generation
Data editing
Data base maintenance
Report generation
Terminal and line control
Restart and recovery
Resource utilization accounting
Performance monitoring
Dump/restore
Job status inquiry
Demand inquiries

DATA DESCRIPTIONS

The data descriptions section describes in detail the files, tables, data elements, and records that comprise the data base. Files are logical collections of related records. File structures vary widely in format and content with designer concepts and the requirements of specific data management systems. This section indicates the following information about each file comprising the data base:

Tag/label
File name
Narrative file description
File creation method
Number of records
Update frequency
Method of update
File contents
Formats of records
Accessing methods
Authorized users
Security requirements
Backup requirements
Storage media
Program using file
File control information

Tables contain reference data that are utilized by various programs. Each table should be described as follows:

Tag/label
Table name
Narrative table description
Functions of table
Number of entries
Method of update
Table contents
Format of entries
Programs using table
Table control information

Data elements are discrete units of detailed information occupying specific positions within tables or records. A record is usually a collection of one or more data elements. Data element definition should include:

Tag/label
Item name
Narrative item description
Function of item
Table/record location
Position of item
Format of item
Values of item

Each record or entry in the files and tables comprising the data base should be defined as follows:

Tag/label
Record name
Narrative description
Function of record
File/table location
Position of record

Format of record
Values of record

STORAGE REQUIREMENTS

This section of the document describes and graphically illustrates the location of programs and data in primary and secondary storage. Programs and tables that will permanently reside in primary memory are identified. All reserved work and buffer areas are specified. A map of primary memory should depict all reserved and working areas. The design logic behind the memory allocation and any constraints associated with it should be stated.

The data storage assignments on peripheral devices of programs and data should be listed and, if appropriate, illustrated. Permanent storage assignments, temporary storage assignments, working areas, unused areas, and reserved areas should be included.

INTERFACE REQUIREMENTS

Requirements to interface this data base with other data bases should be described, and the data that will be exchanged or shared should be identified. Constraints on the sharing of data should be stated.

PROGRAM SPECIFICATIONS (PS)

The program specifications define in detail the computer programs that must be developed, and programmers work directly from them when they write programs. A specification is prepared for *each* program that is to be utilized in the system, and it contains:

A narrative description of the program functions
Input/output requirements
Processing requirements
Macro logic flow charts
Hardware/software requirements
Program interface requirements
Security requirements

Input/output record layouts
Report/display formats

A major concern in producing program specifications is that the specifications be relatively complete and accurate. The programmer should be able to read a program specification and with minimum delay begin to write programs. He should not be required to, in effect, perform a systems analysis and design to determine the program requirements and, thereby, duplicate the work of the system analyst.

If the program specifications are inaccurate, considerable programming effort can be wasted. Attempts to patch and modify faulty program specifications usually produce major data system development cost and time overruns. The program specification is subdivided as follows:

1. Objectives and background
   - Purpose of program specification
   - Project references
2. Program requirements
   - Program performance requirements
   - Program functions
   - Program modification
3. Operating environment
   - Equipment environment
   - Software environment
   - System interfaces
   - Storage requirements
   - Security requirements
   - Controls requirements
4. Detailed design data
   - Operating procedures
   - Inputs
   - Outputs
   - Files
   - Program logic

OBJECTIVES AND BACKGROUND

The objectives of the program specification should be described as follows:

> *This Program Specification for [project name and number] is written to provide:*
>
> - *A working document to guide the programming staff in the development of a specific computer program.*
> - *A review of the requirements and functions of the program.*
> - *A description of the operating environment in which the program will operate.*
> - *Detailed specifications for the computer program to be developed.*

References applicable to the history and development of the project should be included. The project sponsor and user and the data center that will run the completed computer programs should be indicated. The following documents, if they are applicable, should be referenced:

Functional Description (FD)
Data Base Specifications (DS)
Other Program Specifications (PS)
Relevant technical manuals

PROGRAM REQUIREMENTS

This section reviews the requirements and functions of the data system stated in the system/subsystem specification and functional description. The narrative serves to orient the reader to the objectives of the program and the data system of which it is a part.

The functions of the program should be stated and related to the system/subsystem specification. Typical requirements would relate to:

Job throughput time
Response time
Priority levels
Reliability requirements

Expansion capability
Telecommunications requirements
Security requirements

The ability of the computer program to be modified to incorporate changes should be discussed. Changes in the people, machine, and software environments in which the program operates may require program modifications. The capability of the program to accommodate such changes should be described.

OPERATING ENVIRONMENT

This section describes the operating environment: the equipment, software, interfaces, storage, security, and controls necessary for operation of the program. The description should be compatible with that of the data system environment in the system/subsystem specification. Any discrepancies between the two descriptions should be identified and explained. The program interface requirements will include a definition of:

Nature of the interface
Data transfer requirements
Formats and protocols
Responsibilities
Frequency of transfer
Data volumes
Editing and checking requirements
Security requirements

The storage requirements of the program in both primary and secondary should be considered.

The program security requirements will be defined and will include both procedural and operational security. System controls to insure the integrity of processing include:

Limit checks
Arithmetic proof

Identification checks
Label checks
Sequence checks
Record counts
Control totals
Check digits
Special printouts
Audit transactions

DETAILED DESIGN DATA

This section describes operating procedures, inputs, outputs, data environment, and program logic. General operating procedures include program load, initiation, recovery, restart, and completion procedures. Unique program operating requirements also are specified.

The following basic data necessary to describe the program's data flow are included:

Inputs
- Title and tag
- Sources
- Volumes and frequencies
- Formats
- Medium
- Editing requirements
- Time constraints
- Security requirements
- Special handling
- Means of entry
- Priority levels

Outputs
- Title and tag
- Recipients
- Volume and frequencies
- Formats
- Medium

Editing requirements
Time constraints
Security requirements
Special handling
Priority levels

Files

Title and tag
Description
Number of entries
Format
Medium
Security requirements
Update frequency
Retention cycle

The allocation of files in primary and secondary storage is described and illustrated. The data retention cycles of files will be discussed in regard to retention period, storage media, and retrieval requirements. The relation between the program and data base files will be described.

This section also contains a macro logic flow of the program; the flow chart illustrates the overall logic of the program and its major modules. A narrative description usually accompanies the macro flow chart. The major logic modules and the functions satisfied by the modules are represented. The functions being satisfied should relate to the functions described in the system/subsystem specifications.

SUMMARY

The output from the design phase of a project is a detailed design report. For more complex projects, the contents of the report may be modularized to system/subsystem specifications, data base specifications, and program specifications.

The system/subsystem specification represents a level of detail beyond the functional description; it expands the system requirements stated in that description. Changes to the requirements contained in the functional description should be clearly identified. The document is prepared prior to the actual programming of the data system.

In preparing a system/subsystem specification and its detailed system specifications, the following elements should be considered:

Sources of data
Destinations
Data formats
Information volumes
Message frequencies
Response time
Reliability
System balance
Data editing
Security
Performance monitoring
Exception reporting
Cost

The designer of a system must seek to achieve a balance of system components. The elements that he must balance to avoid system bottlenecks are:

Central computer
Communications multiplexer
Data sets
Communications facility
Concentrators
Terminals

The data base specification describes the system files, tables, and directories. The document is prepared when the data system has significant file structuring, accessing, and maintenance requirements. It is intended to be used by programmers and data base administrators.

Data management systems have been developed to simplify the implementation and operation of information systems. They differ primarily in language utilized, file organization and access methods, and level of system users. In addition to describing relevant data management software, the data base specification describes in detail the logical and physical structures of the data base. The location of programs and data in primary and secondary storage is graphically illustrated.

A program specification defines in detail a computer program to be developed. A separate specification is prepared for each program. Programmers work directly from the specifications when writing computer programs. Each specification contains the following:

Input/output requirements
Processing requirements
Macro logic flow charts
Hardware/software requirements
Program interface requirements
Security requirements
Input/output record layout
Report/display formats

A prime consideration is that program specifications be complete and accurate. The programmer should be able to read a program specification and with minimum delay begin to write the required program.

6.

Development

Several management techniques for increasing computer programmer productivity and control programmer work quality are discussed in this chapter. The application of these techniques—chief programmer teams, structured programming, and top-down development—can reduce the time and cost of developing an information system. This chapter and its emphasis on the management of programming work is of special interest to policy and middle management, who have traditionally regarded programming as a mysterious art. The manager of data processing is provided with a review of these programming techniques, sometimes referred to as improved programming techniques, and also a discussion of program documentation requirements during the development phase.

During the development phase of a project, the program specifications prepared during the design phase of application development are utilized by programmers to write computer programs. The development phase falls between the design and implementation phases. During it, errors and deficiencies in earlier phases usually show up. Those deficiencies can result in project delays, inadequate program testing, and disappointing program performance.

CHIEF PROGRAMMER TEAMS

As systems have become more complex with real-time applications and integrated data bases, management of the programmer function has become increasingly difficult. It is often confronted by problems related to individual programmer productivity, software reliability, the slippage of software delivery dates, and program documentation. Often there is an interrelation between those problems that complicates effective management action.

Programmer productivity is measured by the amount of efficient program code that a programmer can produce in a specific period of time. Productivity is influenced by such factors as the programming language being used, programmer experience, on-line versus off-line programming, the stability of the data system design, the number of subprograms, the use of different computers for program development and operation, the use of random access storage devices, the availability of computer test time, programmer morale, and the quality of the programming specifications given to the programmer. The production variation between individual programmers of comparable education and experience is dramatic. However, the problem of improving programmer productivity is complicated by the number of factors that can influence productivity.

The software reliability problem manifests itself in the form of bugs or errors that appear after a supposedly tested program is put into production. Many of the reliability problems result from poor design and inadequate program testing; others arise from improper software maintenance and modification. When programs are poorly documented, programs are inefficiently designed, and personnel turnover is high, new errors will be introduced during the maintenance and modification of the operational programs.

A chronic problem in the data processing industry is slippage in software delivery dates. Because of inadequate project control methods and poor estimating techniques, many programming projects begin with totally unrealistic time schedules. Delays in the implementation of systems relate to the difficulty of establishing programming productivity standards and measuring programming work progress. Systems are becoming more and more complex as more data systems require on-line information and integrated files. Potential problems that can affect a data system increase dramatically when complex data systems are developed. Such problems tend to be more visible and irritating to top management, the intended users of these information systems.

Management's ability to allocate manpower to a project effectively is compromised by the lack of programmer productivity yardsticks. Poor project control by management, combined with fallacious estimating techniques, produces late software. Management often imposes arbitrary software delivery dates on programming personnel before the data system specifications have been finalized. Programmers, in turn, tend to be overly optimistic in estimating program development time requirements and often underestimate design and testing complications.

As projects slip behind schedule, documentation suffers. Management and user pressure on the programming staff to meet the scheduled date for program operation usually results in skimpy program documentation. The quality of the narrative descriptions, test results, program listings, logic flow charts, and other documentation that support the program is sacrificed to expedite the development of the program. The poorly documented program that finally becomes operational will be difficult to operate, maintain, and modify.

Firm control of data systems projects is necessary to minimize these problems. Control requires careful planning, realistic time and cost estimation, and work milestones or checkpoints. Programming management must recognize the need for such controls, be willing to test new control techniques, and firmly support the controls established for a data systems project.

Structured programming is a technique for improving management control of the programming function and increasing programmer productivity. Management control is increased because structured programming simplifies the structure of programs. The concept of structured programming is usually related to the associated concepts of chief programmer team organization with a development support library and top-down data system development. Although structured programming, chief programmer team organization, and top-down development are technically independent techniques, they are often combined during a data system development effort.

The chief programmer team concept seeks to improve programmer organization and improve the efficiency and reliability of finished programs. A team is a small group of personnel organized into a programming unit; a typical one consists of from three to five programmers, a librarian, and several specialists. It is estimated that a chief programmer team can produce a medium-size data system with approximately 25,000 lines of source code in a 12- to 18-month time span.

The nucleus of the team is composed of a chief programmer, a backup programmer, and a librarian. The chief programmer identifies additional personnel to be added to the nucleus. He assigns program production responsibility to individuals with the required experience and skills. The librarian maintains the current status of programs and test data and thereby reduces the clerical workload carried by the programmers. The team could, in the development of large data systems, be assigned responsibility for development of one specific subsystem, and it can, therefore, be integrated into more traditional management organization structures.

The chief programmer is supported by specialists. The backup programmer supports him at the technical design level; the librarian supports him at the clerical procedures and data-handling level. Other programmers on the team are assigned specific tasks by the chief programmer. Specialists are added to the team by the chief programmer to provide specific skills. The framework necessary for the chief programmer team usually includes:

Support by management
A clear definition of team responsibilities

Specialization of program development functions
Skilled team members
Top-down system development
Career paths for team members

Each member of the team should act as a super programmer, and the team should consist of members with the skills and experience necessary to develop the data system. The lines of communication of the team should be short, and the team should have great continuity and awareness of team objectives.

Programming productivity is improved by reducing the time necessary to correct program design errors and debug programs. The unity of design understanding by team members simplifies both program design and program coding. Structured programming modularizes and controls the development or programming process. The competence and motivation of the team members result in faster and more efficient code production. The end result should be improved programmer productivity and more efficient and reliable operational data systems.

The chief programmer is the technical project manager responsible for the success of the programming effort. He codes critical segments of programs and defines program stubs for other team members. He reviews the work of other team members for quality and completeness. He must also motivate team members and insure that communication between them is satisfactory.

The backup programmer should possess as much familiarity with the project and its objectives as the chief programmer. He should be a peer of the chief programmer and also work directly on project programming tasks. If necessary, he should be able to substitute for the chief programmer. Ordinarily, however, the chief programmer can utilize the backup programmer to test management strategies, implement program design concepts, and manage specific tasks. By delegating some responsibilities to the backup programmer, the chief programmer can concentrate on critical development tasks.

The librarian maintains the development support library (DSL), for the contents of which the chief programmer is responsible. The library is a set of office and machine procedures that standardize and control the secretarial, clerical, key-punching, and machine operations necessary to support the chief programmer team. The office procedures are employed to create input to the machine procedures from programmer-produced material and also to file output from the machine procedures in project notebooks and the archives of the external library.

The office procedures are clerical rules used by the programming librarian for accepting directions marked in the external library by the programmers, filing updated status listings in the external library, and filing pages in the archives. The machine procedures are standard instructions for updating libraries, retrieving modules for compilations, linkage editing of jobs and test runs, backing up and restoring libraries, and generating library status listings. Both machine-readable (internal) and human-readable (external) libraries are maintained. The internal library contains such programming data as source code, linkage editing statements, object modules, job control statements, and test information. The external library contains current listings and archives consisting of old listings.

Notebooks that are maintained by the librarian contain directories and alphabetized lists of the modules comprising the data system. The notebooks indicate the status of each module. The directories and member modules that are updated and removed from the notebooks are filed in chronological journals for historical reference. The results of all module tests are also filed in chronological journals.

Programmers change the project status by writing programs or data on coding sheets or by making corrections in the DSL status notebooks. The machine procedures maintain the internal library data on a disk file. Programmers can alter project status only in the external library; they have no direct access to the internal library except through the librarian. The librarian updates the external library as programmers write programs or data on coding sheets and then schedules the programs for execution and updates the internal library. The output from the execution goes to the external library, and the data that it replaces go to the archives.

The librarian schedules all assembling, compiling, linkage editing, and test runs required for the project. Project control documentation also is maintained by the librarian; it consists of the work plans, time schedules, manpower assignments, and cost reports that define the projected and actual status of the project. The librarian maintains the status of programs and test data with procedures that increase programmer production and program reliability. The DSL structure makes the output produced by team members visible and improves communication between team members. The chief programmer and other programmers are freed from many clerical operations and can devote more of their time to programming activities.

STRUCTURED PROGRAMMING

The complexity of programs is often caused by jumps forward and backward in the program code, and the jumps can make it difficult for the reader to follow the logic of a program and track the program segments that have been executed. Program changes or modifications can insert additional jumps that further decrease the readability of the program. During its life cycle the program becomes increasingly difficult to understand and maintain.

Structured programming is based on the principle that any computer program having one entry point and one exit point can be reduced to a form consisting of no more than the three basic control structures illustrated in Figure 6-1. The box symbols represent program functions; the diamond symbols represent true-false decisions; and the circle symbols represent logical connectors. The three control structures are simple sequence, selection, and repetition, and Figure 6-1 shows the basic structures nested within each other to construct a complex logic flow chart. The logic structure of the complex program does not contain arbitrary branching in the form of unconditional branches or statement labels to which to branch.

Programs can be read from top to bottom without unconditional branches and are therefore much easier to read and comprehend. The simple structure facilitates the development and execution of test cases

Figure 6-1. Nesting of control structures.

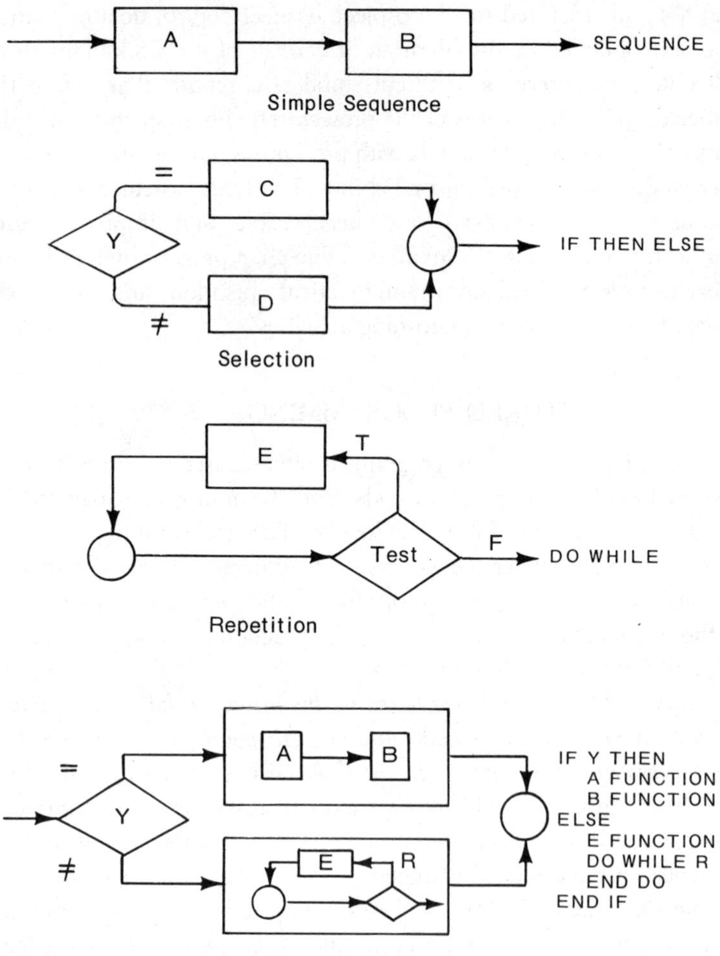

to debug the program. The programmer writing structured programs can be compared with the engineer designing computer logic. The engineer utilizes Boolean algebra that permits complex logic functions to be expressed in terms of *and*, *or*, and *not* operations. The elimination of unconditional branches or GO TO statements simplifies analysis of the program. One can read a program in logic sequence without unconditional branches and quickly define the logic necessary to make a program modification.

Indentation conventions or rules have been developed so that indentation corresponds to logic level as illustrated by the nested flow in Figure 6-1. The indentation of program statements makes the program structure more obvious to the reader. By utilizing descriptive identifiers, a programmer can reduce the need for lengthy descriptive comments and thereby simplify program documentation.

In structured programming, conventions define the length of individual blocks of source code. The effort of modular programming is to divide a program into independent modules. Typically, blocks will not exceed a single listed page or approximately fifty lines. The objective of the size constraint is to modularize the logical components of a program to simplify testing and program understanding. The benefits of modular program design are:

- The simplicity of the program structure improves programmer productivity.
- Programming errors are reduced because the structure of the program is simplified.
- Testing is easier because modules are relatively independent.
- Project control is increased by subdivision of work into discrete segments.
- Reusable modules that can be used as building blocks in more than one program can be constructed.

The modular structure of the program simplifies program testing and permits testing at a relatively early stage in data system development. Dummy subroutines can be utilized to represent unavailable program modules.

Both the program segment size limitation and the indentation rules to improve logic clarity are intended to improve control over program complexity and thereby improve management of the programming function. ALGOL, PL/1, and JOVIAL have a block structure and are highly adaptable to structured programming. Low-level assembler languages are adapted to structured programming by means of macros that introduce and delimit blocks and provide DO WHILE and IF THEN ELSE functions. COBOL can be adapted by limiting programmers to a subset of the language and permitting the use of GO TO only on a special basis.

TOP-DOWN DEVELOPMENT

The technique of top-down development requires that programming and implementation of the data system proceed in a top-down fashion. Program stubs simulate modules not yet developed.

Top-down systems development follows the natural sequence of systems design and requires that programming proceed from the control (interface) architecture and basic definitions downward to the functional units in the system. This process produces the continual integration and testing of systems components as they are programmed and defines interfaces prior to subsystems being developed.

Traditionally, programming techniques provide for general programming systems design but then implement from the bottom up. Subsystems are written and integrated into higher levels of the final data system. This process complicates problem isolation because of the large number of potential problem sources. Management control has limited effectiveness because there is no substantial product until several integrations have occurred.

As illustrated in Figure 6-2, the progression of program development in top-down development is job control, linkage editor, and main program code. New program modules are always added to a debugged program. The supervisor programs are tested early in the development cycle and utilize dummy program modules. The chief programmer has specified the programming design structure, and he oversees and checks modules that are produced by programmers on the project team.

Interfaces in each subsystem are defined prior to program development. Data base definition statements and sample data records are generated prior to program testing. The data base interfaces and calling sequence parameters are also defined in a top-down fashion, which permits a great simplification of the program development process. With a top-down development effort, individual program modules to perform specific functions tend to evolve naturally, which simplifies program testing and debugging. In addition, because the sys-

Figure 6-2. Top-down development phases.

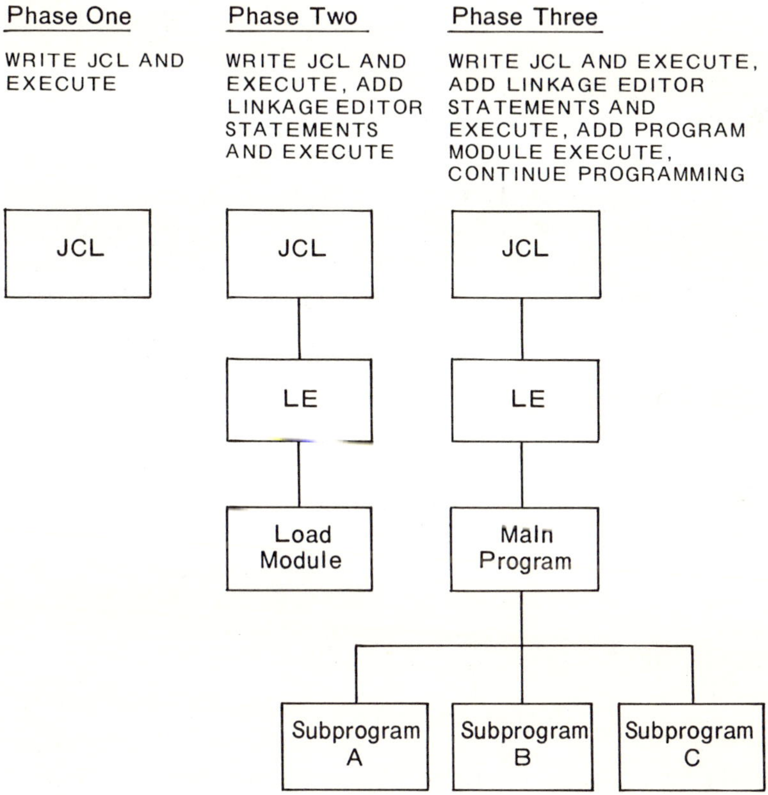

tem is being programmed top-down, the basic design functions of the system should be accomplished and major design imperfections rapidly identified.

The traditional program development process usually produces unplanned difficulties during system testing and integration. It is often difficult to isolate a problem during the traditional integration cycle because of the large number of potential sources. The result is project delays because of program modifications and problem tracing and isolation. Management control often is ineffective during much of the traditional development cycle because there is no coherent, visible product until integration. These difficulties are minimized by top-down development.

A method known as Hierarchy plus Input, Process, and Output (HIPO) is one way of graphically depicting a software system in a top-down fashion. HIPO creates a tree-like structure that explodes functions into increasingly lower levels of detail to define all system subfunctions. Each box in the hierarchy has a corresponding IPO diagram that explodes each subfunction into its three components (input, process, and output). The software requirements in HIPO form are defined during meetings attended by the programming team and user personnel.

As HIPO diagrams are completed, user "walk throughs" of the HIPO design are scheduled. Users are asked to start at the top of the hierarchy and proceed downward through each function looking for errors and omissions. The design walk throughs are intended to assure the users that all their requirements have been satisfied and to obtain user agreement that all functions are present and correct.

PROGRAM DOCUMENTATION (PD)

During the development phase, programmers work from the program specifications prepared in the design phase and write and test computer programs. The following steps are followed by programmers during this phase:

Step 1: Review Program Specifications. The programming team reviews the program specifications to determine their completeness and clarity. The functions of the program, the language to be utilized, the input data requirements, the output data requirements, the processing requirements, and operating controls are studied and evaluated by the programming team. The problem must be well defined before the programming team can effectively begin programming.

Step 2: Research Algorithms and Data Structures. The programming team next determines whether algorithms and techniques that can be adapted to the program to be developed already exist. If well-documented and tested algorithms can be located and utilized, programming time can be reduced. The data base requirements stated in the program specifications will also be researched, and the data structure for the program will be selected. For example, a linked list structure might be selected.

Step 3: Define Logic Structure. The programming team will next segment the program to be developed into basic modules. Macro flow charts can be utilized to describe the main logic flow of the program visually. After the macro flow charts have been constructed and checked, micro flow charts, as illustrated in Figure 6-3, detail the logic flow of the program. If structured programming techniques are being employed, only three logical constructions are allowed: simple sequence, selection, and repetition. Standard symbols and forms should be used in constructing the macro and micro flow charts. Decision tables can also be used to represent the logic structure of the program.

Step 4: Program Coding. The programmers next work from the micro flow charts and code the program. Mnemonic names and labels should be selected for clarity. The names chosen for variables also should be selected to convey an indication of the meaning of the quantity to a reader. Indentation on the coding sheets can be so em-

Figure 6-3. Logic flow chart.

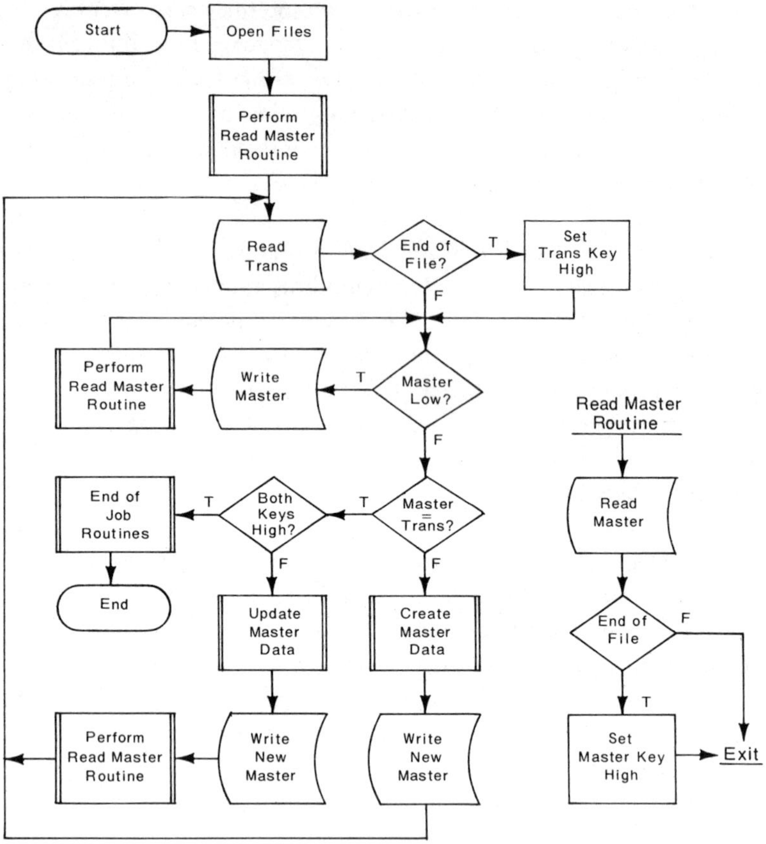

ployed that it corresponds to the logical depth of the statement. Comments should be used to illuminate potentially confusing sections of logic code. The objective of coding should be to produce a well-organized, neat, and readable program code.

Step 5: Desk-Check and Compile. After the logic code has been desk-checked for errors, the program will be compiled. The compiler will list such errors as misspelled variable names, invalid instructions, and undefined variables. The errors detected by the diagnostics in the compiler will be corrected, and the program will be recompiled. All errors should be corrected before the program is recompiled.

Step 6: Program Test. After the program has been successfully compiled, testing will begin. Test data should be run to check the program code. As many paths in the program should be tested as possible. The test data should test input record formats, output report formats, program controls, and edit routines. Tracing can be effective in isolating errors in that after the execution of each instruction the contents of relevant registers are displayed to the programmer. If top-down design techniques are being employed, higher-level modules can be tested with dummy lower-level modules representing modules in development.

Step 7: Documentation. After the program has been tested, the programmers should finalize documentation. The documentation should have the following content:

1. Objectives and background
   - Purpose of program documentation
   - Project references
2. Program description
   - Narrative description
   - Program functions
   - Environment
3. Design data
   - General operating procedures
   - Input layouts
   - Output layouts
   - File layouts
   - Processing requirements
4. Logic structure
   - Macro flow charts
   - Micro flow charts

5. Test results
   Testing procedures
   Test data
   Verification procedure
6. Program list
   Annotated program list
   Label and symbol tables

OBJECTIVES AND BACKGROUND

This section will describe the purpose of the program documentation as follows:

> *This Program Documentation for [project name and number] is written to provide:*
>
> - *A program description in enough detail to permit program operation and maintenance.*
> - *Documentation of program logic.*
> - *Program test descriptions and results.*
> - *An annotated list of the operational program.*

A brief review of the history of the project should be included. The project sponsor and user and the data center that will operate the programs should be identified. The following documents should be referenced when applicable:

Functional Description (FD)
Data Requirements Document (DR)
System/Subsystem Specifications (SS)
Data Base Specifications (DS)
Related Program Specifications (PS)
Technical manuals

PROGRAM DESCRIPTION

The program description restates the requirements contained in the program specification, and any deviations should be discussed in detail. The description orients the reader to the objectives of the program. The overall purpose of the program and the program's place within the data system are described. The programs that prepare input data and those that receive data created by the program are identified.

The functions of the program as they relate to throughput time, response time, and telecommunications capability are stated. They should be consistent with those contained in the program specification. Next, the environment in which the program will operate should be discussed. The discussion should review support software, interface, storage, security, and control requirements.

DESIGN DATA

The general operating instructions and procedures of the program, including program load, recovery, and completion instructions, are stated. Program deck structures, data deck structures, and error messages should be described.

Each input data record will be identified. Layouts of the format and the contents of each record will be drawn. The following information will be provided:

- Title and tag
- Sources
- Volumes and frequencies
- Formats
- Medium
- Editing requirements
- Time constraints
- Security requirements
- Special handling
- Means of entry
- Priority levels

The output in the reports, terminal printouts, and displays of the data system should be depicted in layouts. Output descriptions will include the following information:

Title and tag
Recipients
Volume and frequencies
Formats
Medium
Editing requirements
Time constraints
Security requirements
Special handling
Priority levels

File descriptions should include the following information:

Title and tag
Description
Number of entries
Format
Medium
Security requirements
Update frequency
Retention cycle

The processing structure of the program should be described as follows:

Data manipulation and mathematical calculations
Reference tables utilized and matrices generated by program
Logic procedure for handling exception conditions
Standard subroutines being utilized

LOGIC STRUCTURE

This section should contain macro and micro logic flow charts of the program. A flow chart is a graphic representation of the processing procedures in the program. Symbols represent operations and the order in which they are sequenced. The macro flow chart presents the general logic structure of the program in terms of its primary modules.

It should be accompanied by a narrative description. The micro flow chart depicts the detail logic flow of the program. The programmer will work directly from the micro flow chart when completing the program coding sheets.

TEST RESULTS

This section of the program documentation describes program test techniques and procedures. It should include lists of test data and results and a description of verification procedures. The extent of program testing should be indicated, and any program deficiencies should be uncovered during testing. Any assumptions that have affected testing or test results should be stated.

PROGRAM LIST

A clean, annotated list of the tested program should be included in this section. The list should be sequence-numbered. Relevant lists of label and symbol tables should also be included.

SUMMARY

During the development phase of a project, programmers work from the program specifications prepared during the design phase and produce operational programs. Management of programming is often confronted by problems related to programmer productivity, software reliability, the slippage of software delivery dates, and program documentation. Poor project monitoring and control by management combined with fallacious work-estimating techniques produce software projects that overrun time and cost estimates.

Structured programming is a technique that can improve management control of the programming function and increase programmer productivity. It is usually related to the associated concepts of chief programmer team organization with a development support library and top-down data system development. The nucleus of a chief programming team is composed of a chief programmer, a backup programmer, and a librarian. The chief programmer is the technical project manager responsible for the success of the programming effort. He codes critical segments of programs and defines program stubs for other team members. The backup programmer is a peer of the chief programmer, and he also works directly on project programming tasks. The librarian maintains the development support library (DSL), which is a set of office and machine procedures that standardize and control the secretarial, clerical, key-punching, and machine operations necessary to support the chief programmer team. Programmer productivity is improved by reducing the time necessary to correct program design errors and debug programs. The unity of design understanding by team members simplifies both program design and program coding.

Structured programming is based on the principle that any computer program having one entry point and one exit point can be reduced to a form consisting of no more than three basic control structures: simple sequence, selection, and repetition. The logic structure of a structured program does not contain arbitrary branching in the form of unconditional branches or statement labels to which to branch. Programs can be read from top to bottom without unconditional branches and are therefore much easier to read and comprehend.

Top-down development requires that programming and implementation of the data system proceed in a top-down fashion with program stubs simulating the presence of modules not yet developed. Top-down systems development follows the natural sequence of systems design and requires that programming proceed from the control (interface) architecture and basic definitions downward to the functional units in the system. The process produces the continual integration and testing of systems components as they are programmed and defines interfaces prior to subsystems being developed. That permits a great simplification of the program development process. A method known as Hierarchy plus Input, Process, and Output (HIPO) can be used to graphically depict a software system in a top-down fashion. As HIPO diagrams are completed, user walk throughs of the design are scheduled to assure users that all their requirements have been satisfied.

Program documentation should provide the organization with enough detail to operate, maintain, and modify the program efficiently. It should consist of the following elements:

Program narrative descriptions
Input/output layouts
File layouts
Processing descriptions
Macro/micro logic flow charts
Program test procedures and results
Annotated and sequential program list
Label and symbol tables
Operating instructions
Maintenance procedures

7. Implementation

As users of information systems, policy and middle management should be concerned with effective system implementation. This chapter discusses the testing of a system prior to live operation and stresses the importance of good user manuals. The implementation of a system usually requires active user participation and cooperation. This chapter provides the data processing manager with a framework for system testing and an outline for the preparation of user manials.

During the implementation phase, system testing is completed and conversion to the new system is made. System testing follows the program testing completed during the development phase. During this phase, user training also is completed. Users learn to utilize the new data system effectively.

TEST AND IMPLEMENTATION PLAN (TP)

The test and implementation plan contains the orderly schedule of events and list of materials necessary to test and implement the new data systems. The plan defines each discrete level of testing and the objectives of and procedures for each level. A meaningful test hierarchy is constructed as shown in Figure 7-1 to reflect the integration of tested units into progressively more complex groupings. The parts of this document directed toward management or use personnel should be written in nontechnical language, and the parts directed toward computer personnel should be presented in suitable data processing terminology.

Figure 7-1. System testing sequence.

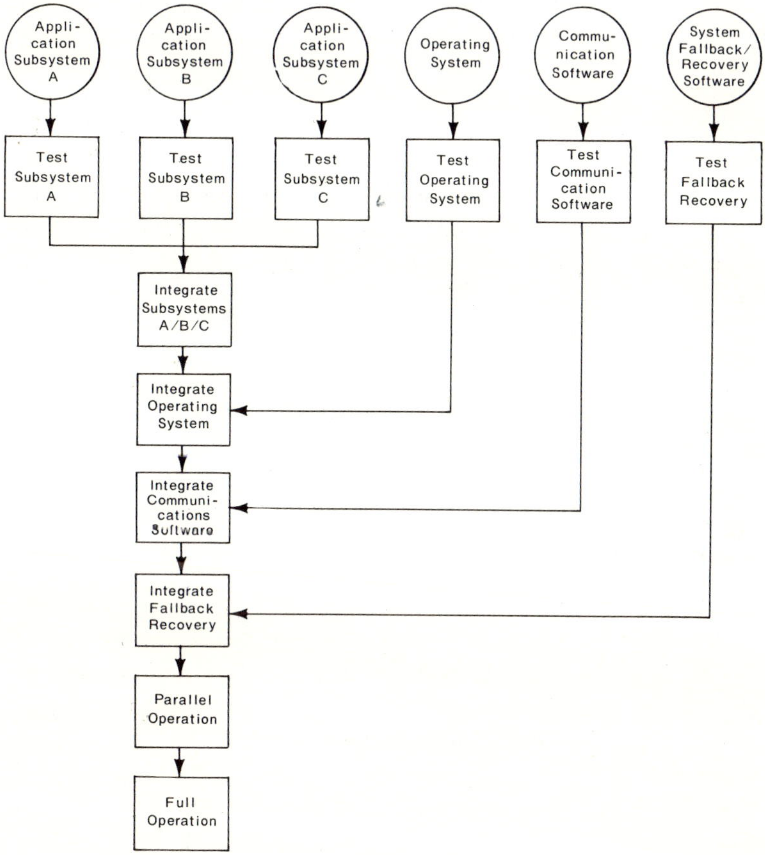

A good data system can be ruined by a poor implementation. Successful implementation usually requires the following:

The support and active involvement of management.
User knowledge of and concurrence with system objectives.
User recognition and acceptance of organizational changes required by the new system.
User recognition and acceptance of responsibilities related to operation and maintenance of the system.
Willingness of the systems analyst staff to create and maintain an atmosphere of mutual respect and cooperation between themselves and the user.

Prior to implementation, management must verify that the system does satisfy defined information requirements, that the equipment, software, and personnel necessary for a successful implementation are available, that control and audit procedures to insure system integrity exist, and that performance requirements have been drafted for evaluation of the operational system.

The actual implementation of a new system can be accomplished by:

- The installation of the new system and the immediate discontinuance of any system and procedures being replaced.
- The phased or modular installation of the new system and the gradual replacement of the old system.
- The parallel operation of the new system with the old system to verify the new system's capabilities and then a discontinuation of the old system.

The immediate, nonphased installation of a new data system without parallel operation is attractive from a resource utilization viewpoint but can be risky. Unless the new system has been thoroughly tested and users are prepared for the approach, implementation problems can be extremely disruptive to the user organization. If the new system encounters unexpected hardware, software, or design difficulties, it may be impossible to fall back to the system that was discontinued.

The phased or modular installation of a new system is attractive because the implementation of each phase can be tightly controlled and the risk to the user organization can be minimized. As each phase or module of the new system operates correctly, the next planned module can be implemented until the entire data system is operational. Usually a major data system—one that cuts across organizational lines and involves numerous organizational components—should be implemented in segments. The implementation may be vertical in the sense of implementing first a production control system, then a marketing information system, and so on or horizontal in the sense of moving up the managerial hierarchy by satisfying the information needs of managers at different levels as implementation work progresses.

The parallel operation of new and old systems permits the comparison of output and performance of the two systems. If the new system has deficiencies, they can be identified and corrected prior to complete cutover to the new system. One difficulty of parallel operation is that the new system may be designed to produce outputs that are difficult to compare with those of the old system.

Another difficulty relates to the manpower and other resources required to run two systems in parallel. Separate controls for the two systems may have to be maintained and reconciled. If difficulties in reconciliation of the systems occur, the period of parallel operation may be prolonged. The delay can place great manpower strains on the user organization because of the requirement to operate two systems. The period of parallel operation should be continued until a predetermined level of performance has been established for the new system. The goal should be to discontinue the old system as soon as possible to avoid the stress of a lengthy parallel operation on the user organization.

Usually it is necessary to either build a data base or convert existing information files into a form usable by the new system. File building or conversion can require significant time and manpower resources. After the data base for the new system has been constructed, it must be maintained. Premature maintenance of files for the new system should be avoided. The maintenance of the files for both the old and new systems can severely strain the manpower in the user organization.

Special programs are often required to validate records being converted prior to their entry into the new data base. If existing records do not contain all the data desired for the new system, a plan to obtain the missing data must be prepared. If the existing files are highly dynamic, then it may be unnecessary to convert them at all. Sometimes existing records can be converted in controllable groups with transaction updates temporarily frozen. During implementation, the user should be requested to develop test data, evaluate test results, and review output formats.

A test and implementation plan should have the following content:

1. Objectives and background
    - Purpose of the test and implementation plan
    - Project references
2. Test overview and schedule
    - System description
    - Test schedule
    - Equipment requirements
    - Software requirements
    - Personnel requirements
    - Training requirements
    - Material requirements
3. System test specifications
    - Performance requirements
    - System function tests
    - Test methodology
    - System test constraints
4. System test descriptions
    - Test sequence
    - Test description

Test inputs
Test outputs
Control information

5. System test procedures
   Test initialization
   Test run
   Completion
6. System test evaluation
   Test evaluation criteria
   Data reduction requirements

OBJECTIVES AND BACKGROUND

The objectives of the test and implementation plan are described as follows:

> *This Test and Implementation Plan for [project name and number] is written for the following reasons:*
>
> - *To provide management with a comprehensive test plan and to provide the user with a description of the steps necessary to implement the new data system.*
> - *To define for the user the schedule of test activities and the equipment, software, and personnel necessary to complete system testing.*
> - *To provide a methodology of testing including test specifications, descriptions, procedures, and deliverable materials.*

A brief summary of references applicable to the background history of the project should be included. The nature of the computer programs to be tested should be defined. In addition, the project sponsor and user and the data center that will use the operational data system should be identified.

The following documents, if they are available, should be cited in the test and implementation plan:

System/Subsystem Specifications (SS)
Data Base Specifications (DS)

Program Specifications (PS)
Program Documentation (PD)

The materials that will be delivered as part of the system should be specified; they include:

System/subsystem specifications
Data base system specifications
Program documentation
User manual, operations manual, and maintenance manual
Operational programs, an operational data base, program listings, and representative system outputs

If applicable, program testing that was accomplished during the development phase should be referenced; descriptions of the program testing are contained in the program documentation. There should be a discussion of any of this program testing that specifically relates to either system testing or operation of the data system.

TEST OVERVIEW AND SCHEDULE

This section should describe the system to be tested and implemented. If the system has subsystems, the relation between the subsystems should be discussed. This overview of the system should be compatible with the narrative description contained in the system/subsystem specifications. System flow charts should be used to depict graphically the flow of data in the system.

A testing sequence as illustrated in Figure 7-2 should be prepared to depict the activities and events necessary to complete system testing and implementation. It should indicate calendar dates, milestones, and the interrelation between activities. The schedule should be approved by both the data processing staff who developed the data system and the user personnel. It should provide milestones for such activities as:

- The completion of all pretest activities including the assembly of test data.

Figure 7-2. System test schedule.

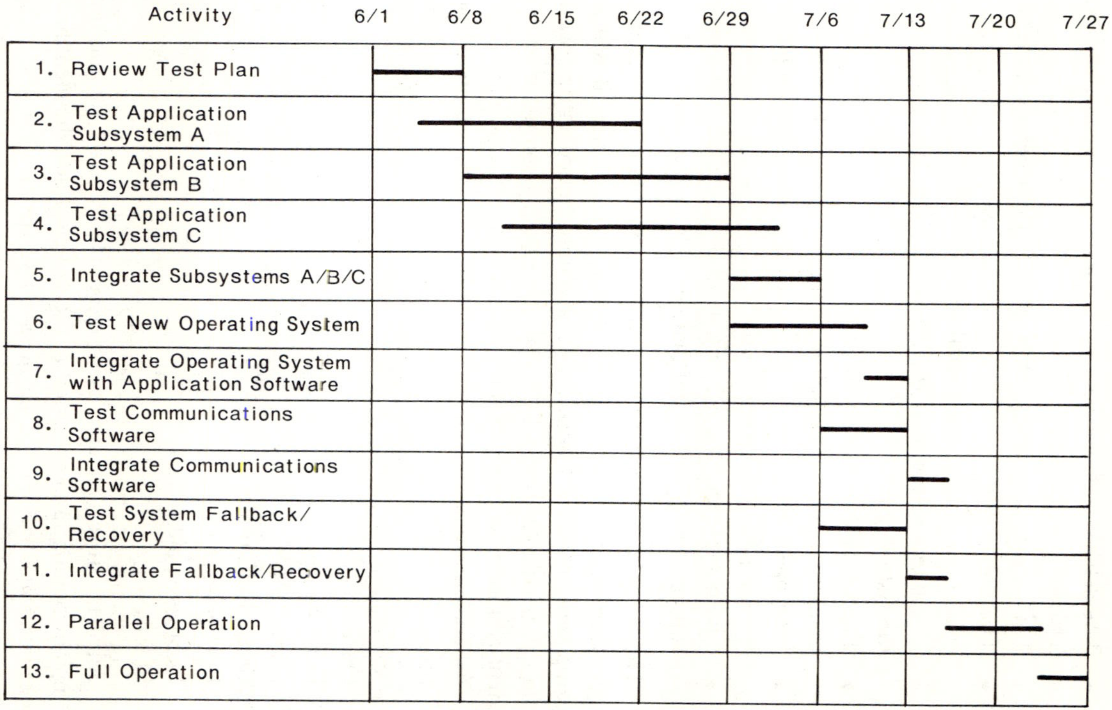

- The delivery and checkout of all equipment necessary for system testing.
- The delivery and checkout of all software necessary for testing.
- The assignment of user personnel necessary to participate in the evaluation of system test results.
- The interpretation and evaluation of the results produced from the system tests.
- The orientation and training of user personnel prior to implementation and live operation of the new data system.
- Live operation of the new data system after the completion of system testing and integration.
- The completion and delivery of all documentation necessary to support the operation and maintenance of the system.

The equipment necessary to conduct testing should be specified by manufacturer, type, and model number. The location at which the equipment must be available and the time period during which it must be available should be stated. Unique and nonstandard equipment configuration requirements should be clearly specified.

All software required for testing should be defined, including the following:

Application programs
Operating system
Data management system
Compilers
Communications software
Data generators
Debugging aids
Simulators

All data processing and user personnel necessary for the testing, implementation, and operation of the system should be identified. An organization chart should be prepared to specify reporting relations and responsibilities. The successful implementation of the data system requires a clear definition of responsibilities.

The plan should also define training requirements. User management must be oriented to the new data system and its capabilities; data preparation personnel must be instructed on data input and correction procedures; and the operation staff must learn the operating and maintenance characteristics of the new system. The training will probably be a combination of classroom and on the job and will utilize the documentation prepared during the implementation and operation phases of data system development.

Materials required for testing and implementation should be identified. Typical materials would be:

Test transaction data
Test data base
Test worksheets
Operator training aids
Data preparation training aids
User management training aids
CPM/PERT charts

SYSTEM TEST SPECIFICATIONS

The performance requirements of the data system should be specified and should be compatible with the requirements stated in the functional description and system/subsystem specifications. The functions being tested should be listed, and the extent to which each function is tested should be specified. Any limitations or constraints that affect function testing should be stated, as should the implications of the constraints.

The methodology of testing should be described. For example, the data system may have been subdivided into subsystems to simplify its development. Each subsystem will be tested at the unit level and then at the system level. The integration of the subsystems will require testing and probably some interface modifications. During the integration of subsystems, the presence of some subsystems that have not been completed might be simulated to expedite testing. The discussion of methodology should also indicate whether the test data and data records represent programmer-produced test data or user-prepared actual data transactions and data records.

The conditions of the test should be described, and discrepancies in transaction volumes, data base size, software, and equipment between the test environment and the data system operational environment should be identified. Data generators, simulators, error detection aids, data reduction routines, trace routines, and similar software that will be utilized to facilitate testing should be listed. Any constraints such as the unavailability of equipment, software, or test data that will limit system testing should be discussed. The effect of these constraints on the quality and completeness of system testing should be discussed.

SYSTEM TEST DESCRIPTIONS

The sequence of steps in system testing should be described. For example, the application programs and operating system might be tested without remote terminals during the early phases of system testing. In later testing phases, communications software and remote terminals would be added to the data system. The more complex elements of the system would be tested in later phases of system testing.

Each test should be described in detail, and the objectives of each should be stated. The data inputs for the test should be described in terms of (1) source of data, (2) type of input, (3) volume of data, and (4) media of input.

The description of data output from the tests should include (1) type of output, (2) volume of output, and (3) media of output.

Test control information should include:

Test readiness indicators
Test progression checkpoint indicators
Test completion indicators
Test failure or irregularity indicators
Destination of test outputs
Priority modes being tested
Test control parameters

Mode of system operation
System console messages during test
Emergency conditions to be tested
Data types and values to be tested
System overload test requirements
Test evaluation criteria

SYSTEM TEST PROCEDURES

This section describes the procedures to be followed during testing. The procedures should guide each test from initialization through test completion. They should also describe test initialization requirements, including the assembly of all test data and the checkout of all test software and equipment. Personnel assignments during the test should be indicated. Test initialization procedures may require the loading of a test data base.

The test run should be described in terms of the sequence of activities and steps. Test run procedures may require periodic data dumps, the visual inspection of test outputs, interim evaluation of test results, or the input of data through the console. The procedures to be followed at test completion should also be described. They will include the collection of test outputs, the recording of system status at completion, the collection of observer notes and observations, and the delivery of outputs to the evaluation team.

SYSTEM TEST EVALUATION

Any test data reduction programs that should be utilized by the evaluating team to reduce or order data for evaluation should be identified. The criteria to be used by the evaluation team in evaluating the system tests should be described. Some typical criteria are:

Validity and accuracy of output reports
Response time of system
Reaction of system to varying processing load
Ability of system to handle different-priority jobs

Multiprocessing capabilities of system
Reaction to emergency conditions
Ease of system operation on operators

TEST ANALYSIS REPORT (TA)

The test analysis report describes the status of the computer system after testing and presents deficiencies for review by management and user personnel. Therefore, the document should be prepared in nontechnical language.

This report documents and creates a formal record of the system tests, which were specified and scheduled in the test and implementation plan. The testing of real-time systems requires significant discipline and test documentation. A complex real-time system will typically be subdivided into subsystems or modules that will be individually tested and then integrated with other subsystems. Figure 7-3 illustrates some of the critical components of a real-time system.

The hierarchical test structure requires management control of test documentation. The test analysis report provides that documentation, and it has the following content:

1. Objectives and background
   - Purpose of test analysis report
   - Project references
2. System test descriptions
   - Test description
   - Performance requirements
   - Demonstrated performance
3. System function tests
   - Test description
   - Function requirements
   - Demonstrated performance
4. System test results
   - System capabilities

Figure 7-3. Critical components of a real-time system.

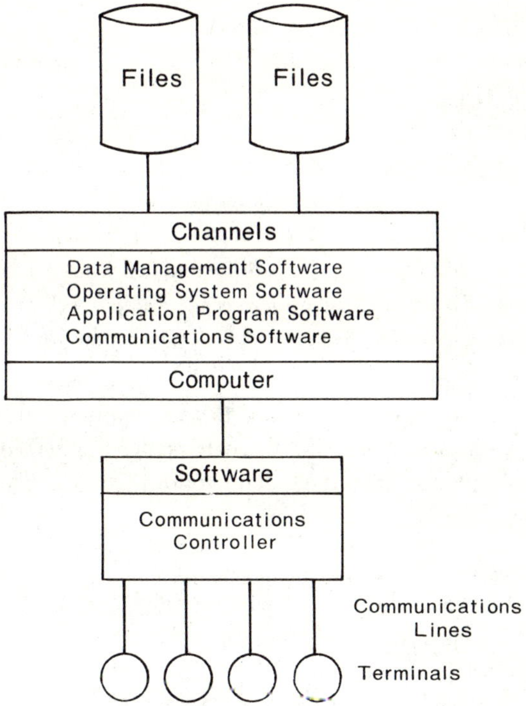

Hardware Utilization

- Central processor
- Primary memory
- Disk/drum storage
- Data channels
- Communications controller
- Communications line
- User terminals

Software Efficiency

- Operating system
- Data management system
- Application programs
- Communications software

Personnel Efficiency

- Computer operators
- Work schedulers
- Quality control staff
- Terminal operators
- Maintenance staff
- Systems programmers

System deficiencies
Recommended actions

OBJECTIVES AND BACKGROUND

This section describes the objectives of the test analysis report in the following terms:

> *This Test Analysis Report for [project name and number] is intended to achieve the following objectives:*
>
> - *To record the results of a specific system test.*
> - *To state system capabilities and deficiencies revealed by the test.*
> - *To establish a basis for system evaluation during testing.*
> - *To provide the user with a document indicating system status.*

Background materials relevant to this report should be cited. The project sponsor and user and the data center that will operate the data system should be identified. The following documents, if they are available, should be referenced:

System/Subsystem Specifications (SS)
Data Base Specifications (DS)
Program Specifications (PS)
Program Documentation (PD)
Test and Implementation Plan (TP)

SYSTEM TEST DESCRIPTIONS

Each performance test should be identified and described. The performance requirements that were tested should be compared with those specified in the test and implementation plan. The test might, for example, be intended for system response time or system reaction to a varying processing load.

SYSTEM FUNCTION TESTS

Each function tested should be identified and described and also compared with that specified in the test and implementation plan.

SYSTEM TEST RESULTS

This section should clearly state the capabilities demonstrated by the system during testing. The statement of capabilities must relate to the required system capabilities stated in the system/subsystem specification and data base specification. Deficiencies revealed by testing should also be described. The effect of each deficiency on required system performance should be discussed. Deficiencies caused by the test environment that would be eliminated in the planned operational environment should be identified. The report should contain an action plan to correct deficiencies, add new capabilities, or proceed to the next step in system testing.

USER MANUAL (UM)

The user manual serves the need of the user group. *It contains general and specific information on the data system and is directed toward general management and user personnel who do not need detailed technical information on the design of the system.* In general, user manuals do not receive adequate attention and are often of marginal quality. Users are simply not given adequate information to utilize a new data system properly. The time allocated to a typical implementation phase does not usually permit user manuals to be produced; typically, implementation time is only 10 percent of the total time allotted to system development.

A major element in gaining user acceptance of a data system is the active involvement of user personnel in the design and implementation process. The technical/company environment in which a data system is designed, developed, and implemented includes not only hardware and software but also business policies, political situations, financial resources, and so on. Successful data processing usually requires that policy and operating management actively support and are involved in it. Then the system becomes their system and they work to insure its success.

If communications problems exist between the computer and user personnel, they usually manifest themselves during the implementation phase and complicate implementation. Conversely, good communication between system development and user personnel can simplify and expedite an implementation.

Data processing management is often so preoccupied with the technical requirements of a data system that psychological and people considerations are neglected. The neglect results in poor communications with user personnel and intensifies user resistance to change. Some user resistance is usually encountered in any case. Data processing management should expect it and plan an implementation strategy that will reduce it to a minimum. Dealing with resistance to change is vital to the successful implementation of a data system.

User personnel may fear that they will be unable to learn the new system and may therefore lose their jobs. User middle management may regard the data system as an intrusion into the traditional way of getting the job done and so may show little interest in it or be skeptical of its capabilities. The new system may appear to them as a threat to their personal control over a functional activity. A new data system may require the reshuffling of responsibilities within the user department. If policy management does not support the new system, organizational changes may create great hostility to it.

User resistance sometimes derives from confusion or misunderstanding. If the system requirements are not explained to the user in advance of implementation or if the explanation is not made by the right person in the management hierarchy, user resistance to necessary organizational changes may block implementation. Resistance to change can be expected if users regard the new system as a threat to their authority or job security.

The installation of a new system requires the extensive training of user personnel. Policy management, middle management, and operating personnel should receive instruction as to system goals and operating procedures. The user manual contains the instructions for the preparation of input data, operation of terminal equipment, and interpretation of output reports by the user staff.

In general, the administrators, supervisors, clerks, and secretaries in user departments do not receive adequate instruction prior to the implementation of new systems and seminars and training classes should be developed to provide them with it. The systems analysts who designed the system and are familiar with its features will normally conduct the training courses because they know the environment in which the system will operate. The user manual should be the primary reference book in these classes.

If user personnel are unfamiliar with or are confused by the data input requirements, operating characteristics, and output formats of the system, they will make errors and question the reliability of the system. They should learn the system and their specific responsibilities for successful system operation and maintenance. If system problems do occur after this formal user training, the systems analyst staff can win user confidence by providing prompt, respectful, and thorough assistance.

The user manual should have the following content:

1. Objectives and background
    - Purpose of the user manual
    - Project references
2. System overview
    - Data system objectives
    - Equipment environment
    - Software environment
    - System interfaces
    - Security requirements
    - Control requirements
3. Detailed operations
    - System inputs
    - System outputs
    - System processing
    - System files
4. System inquiry procedures
    - System inquiry capabilities

Inquiry instructions
Control instructions

OBJECTIVES AND BACKGROUND

The objectives of the user manual should be described as follows:

> *This User Manual for [project name and project number] is written for the following reasons:*
>
> - *To provide user personnel with information necessary to understand and utilize the new data system.*
> - *To provide instruction for user operation of data entry equipment, consoles, and terminals.*

Applicable documents should be referenced. The following documents, if they are available, should be cited:

Functional Description (FD)
System/Subsystem Specifications (SS)
Data Base Specifications (DS)

SYSTEM OVERVIEW

The objectives of the data system should be summarized to provide the user with an overview of the system. The overview should closely correspond to the objectives stated in the functional description and system/subsystem specifications. Organization and system flow charts should be included to depict the system's organizational and data structures. User organizations providing input to the system or receiving output from it should be described. The user activities that are supported by the data system should be clearly identified. All assumptions and constraints that affect system performance should be stated.

The following system performance requirements should be reviewed:

Job throughput time
Terminal response time

Job priority levels
System reliability requirements
System expansion capability
Security requirements

There should be a discussion of the operating environment of the data system necessary to support the system. The required equipment should be described in terms of:

Central processing unit
Secondary storage
Input devices
Output devices
Communications and terminals

A macroschematic diagram of the equipment configuration, if appropriate, should be included.

The software environment should be reviewed, and the required software should be identified by name and version number. The software description should include the following:

Operating system
Data management system
Communications software
Assemblers and compilers
Utility programs
Application software

Interfaces between the data system and other systems should be discussed. The following interface information should be provided:

Nature of the interface
Formats and protocols
Organizational responsibilities
Frequency of transfer
Data volumes
Editing requirements
Security requirements

The system requirements relating to security and privacy should be described and should include:

General administration
Procedural security
Personnel practices
Computer operation
Physical site security
System reliability

The controls required to insure the integrity of the data system should be discussed. Typical controls include the following:

Limit check
Arithmetic proof
Identification check
Label check
Sequence checks
Record counts
Control totals
Check digits
Special printouts
Audit transactions

DETAILED OPERATIONS

This section describes, at a level of detail appropriate for user personnel, the system inputs, outputs, processing, and files. Sample input and output records should be included. The discussion of inputs to the system should include the following information:

Purpose of input
Source of input
Input data formats
Volumes and frequencies
Data entry medium
Data editing requirements
Destination of input

Syntax, punctuations, and format rules that should guide user personnel in the preparation of valid input data should be specified. The following information should be provided:

Valid codes
Valid characters
Valid character combinations
Punctuation rules
Data formats
Sequence requirements
Labeling conventions
Language conventions
Control information

Input layout forms should be included to illustrate input records and formats. Narrative explanations should be keyed to the entries on the forms.

System outputs also should be described. The following information should be provided about each system output received by user personnel:

Purpose of output
Source of output
Output data format
Volume and frequencies
Output data media
Output editing requirements
Destination of output

Specific information permitting user interpretation of output data should be included. The following information should be provided:

Output formats
Labeling conventions
Punctuation rules
Language conventions
Control information

Each type of data output should be illustrated with output layouts or sample forms. Narrative explanations should be keyed to the fields of the layouts and forms.

The processing performed on the input data to produce the various system outputs should be described in nontechnical terms. For example, the system's data manipulation and mathematical calculations and its logic procedures based on specific conditions should be discussed. The system files or data base should be described in summary form to provide user personnel with a basic understanding of the types of information contained in the data system. The following file information should be provided:

Name of file
Basic description
Record formats
File medium
Update frequency
Security requirements
Retention cycle

SYSTEM INQUIRY PROCEDURES

This section describes for the user the file inquiry capabilities of the data system. It contains the user procedures and instructions necessary to retrieve information from the system files. The content and format of inquiry instructions should be illustrated, and they will vary greatly with the specific data system and its supporting software. The procedure or steps required to make an inquiry and retrieve data should be clearly documented. Control instructions necessary for the user inquiry should also be documented and illustrated. Specific operating systems and data management systems require such control instructions.

SUMMARY

During the implementation phase, testing is completed and the data system becomes operational. The documents produced during this phase are the test and implementation plan, the test analysis report, and the user manual.

The test and implementation plan organizes and describes the activities necessary to test and implement the data system. It depicts the integration of tested system components into progressively more complex groupings. The plan defines for the user the schedule of test activities and the equipment, software, and personnel necessary to complete system testing. The successful implementation of a data system usually requires:

The support and active involvement of management.
User understanding of the system and its objectives.
User acceptance of system operational responsibilities and the organization changes required by the new system.
A desire by the systems analyst staff to win customer confidence and support.

A new system can be implemented by immediately discontinuing the old system, gradually replacing phases or modules of the old system, or by running both systems in parallel until the new system is reliable enough to replace the old system. In selecting an implementation strategy, recognition should be given to the strain that a conversion places on the resources of the user organization. For example, the premature conversion and maintenance of system files should be avoided.

The test analysis report documents and creates a formal record of the system tests that are specified in the test and implementation plan. The results of each test are recorded with the capabilities and deficiencies revealed by the test. The report should contain recommendations to correct deficiencies, add new capabilities, or proceed to the next step in system testing.

The user manual contains information about the data system necessary for general management and user personnel. It provides the user with information and instructions necessary to understand and utilize the system. For example, it contains instructions for user operation of data entry equipment, consoles, and terminals. In general, user manuals and user personnel training receive inadequate attention and are often of marginal quality. The deficiency is serious because good communication between data processing and user personnel is vital to the success of a data system. If user personnel do not have a satisfactory user manual and are not adequately trained to operate the new system, they will make errors and question the reliability of the system.

The installation of a new data system may encounter resistance to change in the user organization. User personnel may fear the new system and regard it as a threat to their job security or authority. That resistance to change may result in their showing little interest in the new system or their being skeptical of the system's capabilities. Quality user manuals and adequate training can reduce this resistance to change. Data processing management should expect the resistance and attempt to select an implementation strategy that will win user confidence and minimize frictions with the user organization.

8.

Operation

Policy and middle management are provided in this chapter with a review of the documentation necessary to insure the reliable live operation of an information system. The need for system evaluation is also discussed. Good management requires an evaluation of the operational system and a comparison of system live performance with design specifications. The data processing manager is provided with an outline for the key documents to be produced during the operation phase.

After the data system has been fully tested, user personnel have been trained, and conversion has been completed, the system becomes operational. An operations manual details system operations procedures for the computer operations staff, and a maintenance manual specifies requirements for system maintenance. The operational system should be compared with the system specifications contained in the functional description and the system/subsystem specifications. The analysis is summarized in an evaluation report.

OPERATIONS MANUAL (OM)

The efficiency and motivation of the computer operations staff, the method by which the data system is scheduled for processing, and the reasonableness of computer processing charges affect user satisfaction with an operational data system.

The operations manual, which is usually prepared by a programmer, provides computer operations personnel with a detailed description of the computer application and the procedures necessary to operate the application properly. The manual contains setup procedures, work scheduling, control procedures, data retention schedules, priority requirements, and similar control and procedural information. A well-written operations manual will minimize operator errors and reduce job rerun time. A high job rerun rate, assuming the equipment and software are operating properly, usually indicates poor operations manuals, low operator morale, or high operations personnel turnover. Continual job reruns and operational errors that produce delayed or erroneous system outputs rapidly produce user dissatisfaction. Figure 8-1 depicts a typical production cycle for a batch data system.

In general, the training of operators is performed on the job. The complexity of many existing telecommunications computer environments increases the need for more formal training of operators with periodic refresher courses. Operations is often a neglected branch in the data processing department characterized by low morale and high personnel turnover.

Figure 8-1. Batch work flow.

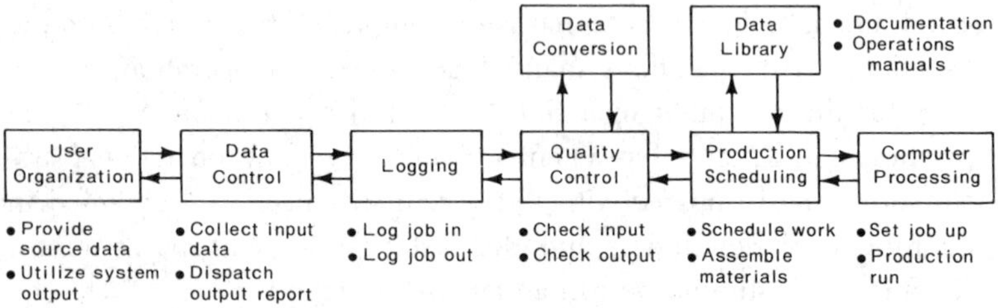

The manager of a data center should be striving to obtain maximum utilization of his resources and provide service to each job in relation to its importance while assuring that each user job is completed within a reasonable time. How the data system is scheduled to run on the computer system, assuming that the system is not permanently resident in memory, can directly affect user satisfaction with the performance of the operational data system.

Job scheduling on a computer system involves both external and internal scheduling. At large data centers a specific production group is usually assigned the task of job scheduling. The group assigns priorities to jobs and determines when each job will be put into the computer. The usual attempt is to mix process-bound and input-output-bound jobs to optimize utilization of the computer resources.

Internal scheduling is the responsibility of the operating system. The data system that is now operational will be controlled by operating system software resident in the memory of the computer system. The operating system controls all the programs running on the computer including the file management software, user programs, utility routines, and all other software routines. It also schedules jobs to be processed and controls the allocation of computer resources. An operating system will typically have to support such functions as:

Maintenance and updating of data files
Query of data files
Program development and debugging
Program initiation and entry into job stream
Generalized mathematical and logical computation
Priority assignments and job scheduling

Some specific capabilities that may be required of an operating system for a computer in a communications environment are the following:

1. Control and coordinate all hardware and associated software.
2. Control interactive user terminals.
3. Monitor batch processing performed concurrently with operation

of remote communications devices and permit users to enter batch jobs into the processing queue from remote terminals as well as the central facility.

4. Priority-schedule user jobs. The scheduling algorithm should be capable of utilizing a number of priority levels. The operating system should be able to recognize the request, schedule it for processing with a specific priority, and transmit the processing results selectively to the appropriate terminal or central facility device.

5. Restart and recover programs that have been suspended automatically or by manual intervention.

6. Verify that data transmission between the computer and remote terminals has been correctly accomplished.

7. Protect programs and data records in core memory or disk storage to prevent unauthorized use or accidental destruction of user programs and data.

8. Provide a time-accounting facility to record at a minimum the day, month, and year, system components used, central processor time, and total elapsed time for any job.

9. Offer a schedule status report on a clock or demand basis and provide at least the following information for each job in the input queue(s): job title, individual job priority, time entered, estimated running time, facilities required.

10. Allow the remote user to query the system to determine the status of his job(s).

The operating system has a scheduler routine that determines when a job will run after it has been put into the computer. Jobs are usually placed in a job queue in secondary storage as they initially enter the computer. The scheduler routine then examines the job queue and determines the next job to enter primary memory. The jobs in primary memory comprise the active job mix, and the scheduler routine determines which of the jobs in the active job mix will next use the central processor.

The internal job scheduling system depends upon the following considerations:

- The priority that has been assigned to the job.
- The resources necessary to execute the job; a large enough block of memory and the necessary peripherals must be available.
- The dependence of the job on the prior completion of other jobs before it can be executed. Other jobs may have to supply data to the job before it can be executed.
- Any reassignment of job priority that has been made by the external operator after the job entered the computer. The operator may initiate on the console a command to the operating system to assign the job a new priority.

Both the external and internal scheduling of jobs must have as their objective the optimal utilization of available system resources. On a system with remote terminals, the terminal user usually assigns a priority to his job and determines when the job will be executed. The job scheduler determines when the job will enter primary memory, how much processor time it will receive, when it will be interrupted, and when the results will be put out or transmitted back to the terminal user. Consequently, the scheduler routine determines system response time, or how rapidly a terminal user will be serviced after he enters a job into the system. Since the satisfaction of terminal users is related directly to system responsiveness, the scheduler routine is a critical element in system effectiveness.

If a data management system is being used, it will be controlled by the operating system and create and maintain user files, edit and translate transaction data, perform file searching and analysis, generate specified output reports, and permit on-line user interrogation of the files. In a network computer environment, the data management software will link the remote terminal user to his files stored at the central computer site. That software will also permit the authorized user to search a file for specific records; actually, it will search the file, analyze the records in the file, and extract the specified records. The user should be able to extract information and reports from his files in defined formats. The software should permit the user considerable flexibility to select data from his files and have an output in a form suitable to his needs.

The job accounting policies and procedures of the data center will also have an impact on user satisfaction with the data system. A number of software accounting packages are available for installation on computer systems. The accounting problem became much more complicated with the advent of third-generation computers that permit more than one program and more than one user to share a computer system simultaneously. Charging for terminals and communication lines further complicates job accounting in that the manager must decide such questions as how to charge for a terminal that is connected to the computer system all day but uses only a few minutes of processing time.

Because of the complexity of third-generation systems, a charge for system overhead must be calculated and prorated among users in addition to operational charges for processing and storage space. The manager must also consider user requests for priority service. Usually a user who requests high-priority service is required to pay a premium for it.

In general, the accounting charges are based on the following criteria:

1. Processor time. The time during which the processor is actually being used; it includes the time during which programs are waiting in core for input or file data.
2. Storage space. The amount and type of storage actually used.
3. Input-output channel time. The time during which the program ties up the channels for retrieving and storing data, reading data, printing data, and/or moving data.
4. Peripheral devices. The time during which the peripheral devices are tied up by a program or job. The time necessary to mount special tapes or put special forms into the printers should be included.

5. Priority level. The priority level assigned by the user to the program.

6. Communication lines. The cost to link user terminals to the central site.

7. Terminal requirements. The cost of acquiring and maintaining user terminals.

8. Proprietary software. The cost of providing proprietary software programs to the user.

One of the considerations in job accounting is whether the time and cost required to track minor costs and bill them to specific users is worthwhile. Job accounting can be cumbersome if carried to a very minute level of billing detail. However, from the user point of view it is desirable to have a complete accounting of computer system charges to be used to relate charges to services received.

The qualifications of the operations staff, the job scheduling methods used, and the job accounting policies of the data center will affect user satisfaction with the operational data system. The operations manual describes the operational requirements of the data system, defines a processing schedule, and specifies the priority level of jobs to be processed. It will usually have the following content:

1. Objectives and background
   - Purpose of operations manual
   - Project references
2. Control procedures
   - General requirements
   - Production schedule
   - Data retention schedule
   - Control forms
3. Operating procedures
   - Equipment requirements
   - Input materials
   - Setup procedures

Computer processing
Output expected
Job completion instructions
Data conversion tasks

4. Nonroutine operations

OBJECTIVES AND BACKGROUND

The objectives of the operations manual are described in the following terms:

> *This Operations Manual for [project name and number] is written to provide the operations staff with:*
>
> - *Detailed instructions on how to schedule, initiate, and process operational programs.*
> - *Information relating to supervisory and clerical review, procedures, data control, and output distribution.*

Relevant background material should be included in this manual. The project sponsor and user and the data center that will run the operational data system should be specified.

The following documents should, if they are relevant, be referenced in this manual: Program Documentation (PD) and Maintenance Manual (MM).

A work flow chart, as shown in Figure 8-2, should be included to depict the sequence of operations necessary to complete the job. It should show the relation between input, processing, and output operations. The operations in the work flow chart should be identified by number and keyed to a narrative description of the operation. The data volumes and timings of each operation should also be specified. The logical phases of work processing in which intermediate results can be checked, such as edit, sort, update, and report preparation, should be identified.

Figure 8-2. Work flow chart.

STEP	DESCRIPTION	RESPONSIBILITY	VOLUME	LATEST TIME IN	LATEST TIME OUT
1	Receive Weekly Pay Source Documents	Data Control	45 Departments Approximately 125 Documents	1200 Thursday	1215 Thursday
2	Check Batches for Completeness	Quality Control	45 Batches	1230 Thursday	1330 Thursday
3	Key-disk Pay Transaction Data	Data Conversion	Approximately 2,500 Payroll Transactions	1345 Thursday	1845 Thursday
4	Check Transaction Tape	Quality Control	1 Payroll Transaction Tape	1900 Thursday	1930 Thursday
5	Assign Run Time	Production Scheduling	N/A	1945 Thursday	2015 Thursday
6	Assemble Files, Transaction Data	Production Scheduling	1 Master File 1 Transaction File	2015 Thursday	2030 Thursday
7	Computer Run Ø1: Transaction, Edit, Run	Computer Operations	1 Transaction Edit List Output	2045 Thursday	
8	Computer Run Ø2: Sort Run	Computer Operations	1 Sorted Transaction Journal Output		
9	Computer Run Ø3: Update Master File	Computer Operations	1 List of File Changes Output		
10	Computer Run Ø4: Computation Run	Computer Operations	1 Exception Journal Output		
11	Computer Run Ø5: Check Printing Rur	Computer Operations	Approximately 2,400 Checks and Stubs		
12	Computer Run Ø6: Print Runs	Computer Operations	6 Output Reports		0700 Friday

CONTROL PROCEDURES

This section will describe the management policies, security requirements, data management procedures, equipment assignments, and similar considerations that control or affect the processing of jobs. If an on-line system is being described, control functions and capabilities of the supervisory and applications software will be described. The following specific information should be included:

The daily, weekly, monthly processing cycle of the job
The receipt, time, and date of input data
The required completion time and date of the job
Operational and data security requirements
Quality control requirements and procedures
Job completion and output delivery requirements

The data retention requirements should be specified and should include the retention period, data release date, and final disposition of the data. The media—tape, disk, paper tape—on which the data are stored, as well as user need for the audit or verification of data and backup requirements, should be considered. Data retained should be identified by system number, run number, and creation date. Relevant control forms also should be described. For example, entries on the request-for-processing form that would be completed by the user should be explained.

OPERATING PROCEDURES

This section of the operations manual specifies in detail the computer and data conversion operations necessary to complete the job. It describes the materials and procedural actions required to schedule, initiate, process, and control jobs in a production state. All job setup instructions, inputs, console messages, outputs, and control procedures are specified. Each operation necessary to complete the job is presented in the sequence normally required in executing the run.

The computer equipment (tapes, disks, memory) and software (operating system version, special software) necessary to complete the run are specified. Input materials required for the run are described. For example, a typical run will require input transactions, master file data, and the application program. The physical form of the input data—punched cards, tape, disk, console input—should be described. The following items also should be described:

The control forms authorizing the run
The content, name, and media of input data
Source of input data and instructions for the handling of input data
Disposition of input data after the run

Job setup instructions on how materials are to be prepared for the production run are provided. Job control instructions that initiate computer processing are precisely identified. Job setup will include loading the necessary computer programs into computer memory and initializing peripheral devices. For example, special forms may have to be loaded into the line printer.

Computer processing instructions should be specified and should include keyboard messages necessary to control the job and messages that indicate error conditions, normal job halts, and abnormal job terminations. Console messages related to the job should be clearly identified, and actions required by the operator in response to a console message should also be identified.

The outputs expected from the run should be described and illustrated. Any verification of the output expected should be indicated. Job completion instruction should specify:

Disposition of each output
Control steps to be performed
Materials to be returned to production control
Corrective actions necessary for each abnormal job termination
Next operation reference if further operations are required
Output binding, labeling, packaging instructions

Data conversion tasks required prior to the computer run should be defined. The definition should include a flow chart of data conversion steps and setup and control instructions.

NONROUTINE OPERATIONS

This section will describe emergency and nonroutine operations. The latter would include switchover to a backup system and recovery from computer hardware or software failure.

MAINTENANCE MANUAL (MM)

Data system maintenance often requires substantial expenditures of time; many data centers have been forced to commit most of their available programming manpower to maintenance tasks. As the number of operational data systems increases, the maintenance workload also increases. The number of programmers available for the development of new data systems can be depleted by the growth in maintenance work. Users can be puzzled by the lack of new data system development at a data center because they do not know the size of the maintenance workload.

If the data system to be modified was poorly documented and then has been patched extensively, maintenance and modification of the system become complex. Even a simple change becomes time-consuming and difficult. Modifying or patching a poorly documented data system is risky because the documentation is unreliable. A minor change might produce unexpected and unwanted results in the operational data system.

System maintenance can result from a change in the organization's policies and procedures (change in fiscal year), a change in programming (a more efficient subroutine), or a change in operating procedures (new hardware or operating system). The change creates a need to modify the data system.

Maintenance should involve both user and data processing personnel. The user organization should approve the system modification, develop data to test the modified system, review the results of the system test, review updates to the documentation, and train user personnel affected by the system modification.

The maintenance manual, which is usually prepared by a programmer who worked on the programming of the data system, describes the data system maintenance requirements. *The manual contains the details and characteristics of each program and subroutine that would be of value to a maintenance programmer in understanding the programs and program relations.* The manual identifies specific procedures that the programmer should follow to maintain the system properly. A maintenance manual typically has the following content:

1. Objectives and background
   - Purpose of the maintenance manual
   - Project references
2. System description
   - System overview
   - Operating environment
3. Detailed program descriptions
   - General description
   - Input data
   - Output data
   - File data
   - Processing structure
4. Program maintenance conventions
   - Maintenance procedures
   - Program testing
   - Documentation of revisions

OBJECTIVES AND BACKGROUND

This section describes the purpose of the maintenance manual in the following words:

> *This Maintenance Manual for [project name and number] is written to provide the maintenance programmer staff with:*
>
> - *Information necessary to maintain and modify the system.*
> - *Procedures, controls, and responsibilities relevant to system maintenance.*

The project sponsor and user and the data center operating the system should be identified. Background materials that would be helpful to the maintenance programming staff should be referenced. For example, the following documents might be referenced:

Operations Manual (OM)
Program Documentation (PD)
System/Subsystem Specifications (SS)
Data Base Specifications (DS)

SYSTEM DESCRIPTION

The objectives and functions of the system should be briefly described to orient the maintenance programmer. For example, if the system to be maintained is a payroll one, the logical components of the system—edit, sort, compute pay, print checks—would be described and the relation between the components specified.

The data system is subdivided into its logical components and the functions performed by each component. Flow charts should be used to depict the relation between the components graphically. The relationship between the computer programs comprising the data system should be specified.

The equipment or hardware environment in which the system is operating should be defined. All software necessary for the operation of the data system—operating system, data management software, communications software—should be identified. The relation of the data system and its programs to other data systems should be stated.

Rules and conventions that apply to the data system, such as programming rules, flow-charting standards, labeling conventions, revision procedures, and testing procedures, should be specified.

DETAILED PROGRAM DESCRIPTIONS

Each program comprising the data system should be listed, and details about each program should then be provided to the maintenance programmer. A narrative description of each program and major subroutine should accompany the listing. The general operating instructions and procedures of each program, including program load, recovery, and completion instructions, should be stated. Program deck structures, data deck structures, and error messages should be described.

Each input data record should be identified, and layouts of the format and contents of each record should be drawn. The following information should be provided:

- Title and tag
- Sources
- Volumes and frequencies
- Formats
- Medium
- Editing requirements
- Time constraints
- Security requirements
- Special handling
- Means of entry
- Priority levels

The data output appearing in the reports, terminal printouts, and displays of the data system should be depicted in layouts. Output descriptions should include the following information:

- Title and tag
- Recipients
- Volume and frequencies
- Formats
- Medium
- Editing requirements
- Time constraints
- Security requirements
- Special handling
- Priority levels

Each file comprising the data system should be described as follows:

Title and tag
Description
Number of entries
Format
Medium
Security requirements
Update frequency
Retention cycle

The processing structure and requirements of the program should be defined in terms of:

Data manipulation and mathematical calculations
Reference tables utilized and matrices generated by program
Logic procedure for handling exception conditions
Standard subroutines being utilized
Storage requirements
Branch conditions in the program
Link to next logical program
Processing completion exit requirements
Error-handling routines
Design limitations on program operation
Associated programs

This section should reference, if necessary, logic flow charts of the program in the appendix of the maintenance manual. The flow charts will show the logical flow of program operations such as read a record, perform calculations, and update a master record. The appendix might also contain source listings of the programs with comments or annotations to explain sections of program code.

PROGRAM MAINTENANCE CONVENTIONS

This section reviews maintenance conventions to insure that the user has approved the modifications and that the modifications are properly tested and adequately documented. Formal procedures for coordinating changes with operations personnel are defined. The operations personnel must approve and understand the maintenance documentation.

EVALUATION REPORT (ER)

The evaluation report compares the operational system with system design specifications and criteria. *The functions and capabilities of the live system are evaluated relative to the requirements stated in the functional description and system/subsystem specifications.* The report seeks to determine whether the live system has met design specifications.

Too few organizations periodically evaluate data systems after the systems become operational. The system evaluation procedure should provide for a comparison of the stated objectives of the system (better service, cost avoidance, improved reporting) with the system's actual performance. Some of the characteristics of a good data system would be:

- User is satisfied with the data system.
- The project to develop the data system was completed on time and at budgeted cost.
- The operational system closely matches the functional description and system/subsystem specifications.
- Testing of the data system was relatively smooth.
- The operational data system is well-documented and simple to maintain.
- User and operations personnel are well trained in their responsibilities.
- The hardware and software used by the data system are well-matched to system requirements.

The evaluation process will reveal both strengths and weaknesses in the data processing organization. The success or failure of a major data system development effort will be determined by such considerations as the extent of policy management involvement, the management practices of the data processing manager, the documents and standards used to control the system development, the skills and motivation of the data processing team, and the involvement of user personnel in the effort.

The evaluation report will typically have the following content:

1. Objectives and background
   - Purpose of the evaluation report
   - Project references
2. System overview
   - Background information
   - System objectives
3. Detailed analysis
   - Performance requirements
   - Data system functions
   - System inputs and outputs
   - File structure
   - System backup and recovery
4. Conclusions
   - Summary of evaluation
   - Recommended actions

OBJECTIVES AND BACKGROUND

The purpose of the evaluation report should be described as follows:

> *This Evaluation Report for [project name and number] is written to:*
>
> - *Determine whether the operational data system has met design specifications contained in the functional description and system/subsystem specifications.*
> - *Compare the actual time and cost required to develop the system to budgeted time and cost.*

- *Evaluate the quality of documentation and user training.*
- *Define unplanned limitations in system performance.*

A summary of the references relevant to the history of the project should be provided. The project sponsor, user, and data center running the operational data system should be identified. The following documents should be referenced:

User Proposal (UP)
Project Plan (PP)
Functional Description (FD)
System/Subsystem Specifications (SS)
Test and Implementation Plan (TP)
Operations Manual (OM)

SYSTEM OVERVIEW

This section should provide a general description of the data system in nontechnical language. Background information that will orient the reader to the objectives of the data system should be included. Related data systems should be identified and the nature of the relation specified. Other capabilities being developed by the organization concurrently with this data system should be described. The objectives of the data system should be specified.

DETAILED ANALYSIS

This section should compare the performance characteristics of the operational data system with the specifications contained in the functional description and system/subsystem specifications. The following elements should be considered:

System response time
Job throughput time
System reliability
Software adequacy
Hardware adequacy

Security features
Audit trail and controls
Accuracy of calculations
System flexibility
Expansion capability
Job priority levels

The functions being performed by the data system should be individually compared with those defined in the system/subsystem specifications. The data inputs and outputs, file structure, processing capabilities, and backup and recovery features of the operational system should also be compared with the design specifications.

CONCLUSIONS
The results of the data system evaluation should be summarized. Unplanned system limitations or constraints should be identified. Specific actions that would enhance the performance or capabilities of the data system should be recommended. The resources and time required to implement each recommended action, as well as the benefits to be derived from each action, should be stated.

SUMMARY

The documents produced from the operations phase are an operations manual, a maintenance manual, and an evaluation report. The operations manual contains a description of setup procedures, work schedules, control procedures, data retention schedules, security requirements, and priority requirements necessary for operation of the data system. User satisfaction with the system will vary with the quality of operations personnel motivation and training, job scheduling policies, and the reasonableness of the data center's accounting system.

Operations personnel motivation and training is often neglected, and operational errors and job reruns are the consequences of the neglect. Job scheduling involves both an external production scheduling group in the operations branch of the data processing organization and the internal job scheduler routine of the operating system software. Scheduling determines system response time and is therefore a critical factor in user satisfaction with system performance. The job accounting system selected by the data center should provide the user with a reasonable level of detail that relates charges to services.

Data system maintenance responsibilities often require extensive programming manpower. If a data system that is to be modified has been poorly documented and extensively patched, even simple changes become complex and time-consuming. A good maintenance manual clearly states the details and characteristics of each program and subroutine in the data system so the maintenance programmer can properly maintain and modify the data system. User personnel should assume maintenance responsibilities related to the approval of changes, creation of test data, review of system test results after the modification, and approval of updates to the data system documentation.

Too few organizations evaluate data systems after they become operational. The evaluation report compares the operational system with the design specifications in the functional description and system/subsystem specifications. The time and cost actually expended on the data system are compared with the estimates in the user proposal and the budgets contained in the project plan. Improvements that could be made to the data system are listed in the evaluation report together with time and cost estimates of each improvement.

9. Conclusion

The rapid technical evolution of computer equipment and software has resulted in a lag in man's ability to manage information system development work effectively. The highly integrated information systems that are emerging involve *all* levels of management—not just the data processing manager. Information systems have become increasingly vital to the operation and survival of many private and public organizations. Management, based on the fact that in most organizations people and software costs now equal or exceed computer hardware costs, must be increasingly concerned with the control of developmental projects and the work performance of computer personnel. A combination of management skill and phased development is necessary for effective information system development.

Policy management is responsible for establishing the goals of the systems and for locating the data processing function in the organizational structure. Middle and operating management, the primary users of the systems, must participate in system design and implementation because their support and understanding will usually determine the success or failure of a system.

The data processing manager requires *both* selling skills and technical competence. He must effectively communicate with policy, middle, and operating management in a language they can understand and explain to them the potentials and limitations of information systems. He must manage technical resources and, at the same time, win user confidence and cooperation. He must motivate and win the loyalty of his own data processing staff. He needs skills in all these categories: leadership, communication, organization, technology, education, and economics.

The successful implementation of information systems requires the following:

- A project control structure to monitor time, cost, and work quality.
- Policy, middle, and operating management's commitment to and active involvement in data processing.
- User knowledge of and concurrence in the objectives of data systems.
- A data processing manager with both leadership and technical skills who can win the support and confidence of users.
- Systems analysts who can communicate with middle management and who understand the organization's applications and operations.
- User recognition and acceptance of user responsibilities associated with the development of new data systems.

The control framework presented in this book consists of six phases and sixteen key documents that can be produced during the design and development of a computer application. This framework should encourage more management control over the time and cost necessary to develop information systems. The use of standard phases and documents should also foster more professionalism in computer application design and development.

The potential of the computer to benefit business, industry, and society relates directly to man's ability to manage the design of information systems. More professionalism in systems design will enhance the ability of organizations to control data processing costs and performance and realize more rapidly the many benefits possible from automation.

Supplementary Reading

Anthony, Robert N., *Planning and Control Systems: A Framework for Analysis*. Cambridge, Mass.: Harvard University Press, 1965.

Bassler, Richard A., and Logan, Jimmie J., *The Technology of Data Base Management Systems*. Arlington, Va.: College Readings, Inc., 1973.

Blumenthal, Sherman S., *Management Information Systems: A Framework for Planning and Development*. Englewood Cliffs, N.J.: Prentice-Hall, Inc., 1969.

Brooks, Frederick P., *The Mythical Man-Month*. Reading, Mass.: Addison-Wesley Publishing Company, Inc., 1974.

Canning, Richard G., and Sisson, Roger L., *The Management of Data Processing*. New York: John Wiley & Sons, Inc., 1967.

Dearden, John, McFarlan, F. W., and Zani, W. M., *Managing Computer-Based Information Systems*. Homewood, Ill.: Richard D. Irwin, Inc., 1971.

Enger, Norman L., *Putting MIS to Work: Managing the Management Information System*. New York: AMA, 1969.

Forrester, Jay W., *Industrial Dynamics*. Cambridge, Mass.: M.I.T. Press and John Wiley & Sons, Inc., 1961.

Head, Robert V., *Manager's Guide to Management Information Systems.* Englewood Cliffs, N.J.: Prentice-Hall, Inc., 1972.

Howerton, Paul W., *Management of Information Handling Systems.* Rochelle Park, N.J.: Hayden Book Company, Inc., 1974.

Kennevan, Walter J., and Joslin, Edward O., *Management and Computer Systems.* Arlington, Va.: College Readings, Inc., 1973.

Krauss, Leonard I., *Computer-Based Management Information Systems.* New York: AMA, 1971.

London, Keith, *Documentation Standards.* Philadelphia: Auerbach Publishers, Inc., 1973.

Martin, James, *Telecommunications and the Computer.* Englewood Cliffs, N.J.: Prentice-Hall, Inc., 1969.

McDonough, Adrian M., and Garrett, Leonard J., *Management Systems: Working Concepts and Practices.* Homewood, Ill.: Richard D. Irwin, Inc., 1965.

Prince, Thomas R., *Information Systems for Management Planning and Control.* Homewood, Ill.: Richard D. Irwin, Inc., 1970.

Schoderbek, Peter P., and Schoderbek, Charles G., *Management Systems.* New York: John Wiley & Sons, Inc., 1971.

Westin, Alan F., and Baker, Michael, *Databanks in a Free Society.* New York: Quadrangle Books, 1972.

Wofsey, Marvin M., *Management of ADP Systems.* Philadelphia: Auerbach Publishers, Inc., 1973.

Glossary

access method A routine external to the application program that performs storage and retrieval of physical data.

access, random A process of obtaining information from or placing information into storage in which the time required for access is independent of the location of the information most recently obtained from or placed in storage.

accounting, job The recording of utilization of system resources by jobs. It permits an assignment of charges for job processing and system operation.

assemble To prepare a machine language program from a symbolic language program.

assembler A program that assembles. (See also *Assemble.*)

assembly language Machine-oriented programming language.

audit trail A means of tracing items of data from processing step by step, particularly from a machine-produced report or other machine output, back to the original source data.

band (communications) (1) The range of frequencies. (2) The frequency spectrum between two defined limits.

bit (1) A single character of a language having just two characters such as the binary digits 0 and 1 (*bi*nary digi*t*). (2) A unit of information storage capacity, as of a computer memory.

branch, unconditional An instruction that switches the sequence of control to some unspecified location. Synonymous with unconditional jump and unconditional transfer of control.

buffer A storage device used to compensate for a difference in rate of flow of data or time of occurrence of events when data are transmitted from one device to another.

bug (1) A mistake in the design of a routine or a computer. (2) A malfunction.

byte A sequence of adjacent binary digits operated upon as a unit and usually shorter than a word. A byte could, for example, represent an alpha character of information. (See also *Bit.*)

channel A path along which signals can be sent, as in a data or output channel.

chart, flow A graphic representation of the major steps of work in process. The illustrative symbols may represent documents, machines, or actions taken during the process.

chart, logic flow A detailed solution of the work order in terms of the logic, or built-in operations and characteristics, of a specific machine. Concise symbolic notation is used to represent the information and describe the input, output, arithmetic, and logic operations involved. The chart indicates types of operations by use of a standard set of block symbols. A coding process normally follows the logic flow chart.

chart, operations flow A schematic representation of the interconnected logic steps necessary to solve a particular problem.

chart, systems flow A schematic representation of the flow of information through the components of a processing system.

check, arithmetic A check that uses mathematical identities, as in checking multiplication by verifying that A times *B* is equal to *B* times A.

check, identification A check procedure that establishes the presence of a symbol or code the purpose of which is to identify, indicate, or name a body of data.

check, label A check that examines a label that identifies an item of data.

check, limit A check based upon known limits defined for items of data.

check, sequence A data processing operation designed to check the sequence of the items in a file assumed to be already in sequence.

checkpoint The act of capturing the state of units of data and the application programs operating on them for the purpose of reconstructing the data and restarting the programs.

COBOL An acronym for COmmon Business-Oriented Language. A specific language by which business data processing procedures may be precisely described in a standard form.

code, source A language code that is an input to a given translation process.

communication, data The transmission of data from one point to another.

compile To prepare a machine language program from a computer program written in another programming language.

compiler A program that compiles.

computing, distributed A decentralized organization of computer systems in which computers are linked together and can share common data.

console The part of a computer that is used for communication between the operator or service engineer and the machine.

control, feedback A type of system control obtained when a portion of the output signal is operated upon and fed back to the input to obtain a desired effect.

conversion The process of changing from one data processing method to another or from one type of equipment to another.

count, record A checking procedure that counts the number of records in a body of data.

cross-talk The interference that results when signals on one telephone circuit appear on another circuit. The circuit that is the source of the signals is known as the disturbing circuit, and that on which the signals are heard is the disturbed circuit.

data Facts, numbers, letters, or symbols of facts that refer to or describe an object, idea, condition, situation, or other factors: the basic elements of information that can be processed in or produced by a computer.

data base A named collection of physical data that are related to each other in a specified manner.

data, test Data developed specifically to test the accuracy of a computer run or system. The data may be actual information that has been taken from preceding operations or contrived information created for this purpose.

debug To isolate and remove mistakes from a routine or a malfunction from a computer.

device, input A mechanical unit designed to bring data to be processed into a computer. Examples are a card reader, tape reader, and keyboard.

device, output The part of a machine that translates the electrical impulses representing data processed by the machine into permanent results such as printed forms, punched cards, or magnetic writing on tape.

device, storage A device into which data can be inserted, in which they can be retained, and from which they can be retrieved.

diagram, block A diagram of a system or program in which selected portions are presented by annotated boxes and interconnecting lines.

diagram, logic A diagram that represents a logic design.

dictionary A list of data names and the intended meanings used in a system.

digit, check A digit used for the purpose of performing a check.

display unit A device that provides a visual representation of data.

documentation The group of techniques necessary for the orderly presentation, organization, and communication of recorded, specialized knowledge. It constitutes a complete record of reasons for changes in variables.

edit To modify the form or format of data, as to insert or delete such characters as page numbers or decimal points.

element, data A specific item of information appearing in a set of data. Examples are the quantity of a supply item issued, a unit rate, an amount, and the balance of stock items on hand.

encrypt To use a cryptographic system in which units of plain text of regular length, usually letters, are arbitrarily transposed or substituted according to a predetermined key.

equipment, off-line Peripheral equipment or devices not in direct communication with the central processing unit of the computer.

equipment, on-line A system and its peripheral equipment or devices under control of the central processing unit.

equipment, peripheral The auxiliary machines that may be placed under the control of the central computer. Examples are card readers, card punches, magnetic-tape feeds, and high-speed printers.

error Any deviation of a computed or measured quantity from the theoretically correct or true value.

evaluation, performance The analysis, in terms of initial objectives and estimates and usually made on-site, of the accomplishments of using an automatic data processing system. The evaluation is intended to provide information on operating experience and identify any corrective actions required.

file A collection of related records. In inventory control, for example, one line of an invoice containing data on the material, quantity, and price forms an item, a complete invoice forms a record, and the complete set of such records forms a file.

file, detail A file of information that is relatively transient.

file, master A file of information that is relatively permanent.

format A predetermined arrangement of characters, fields, lines, page numbers, and punctuation marks. The reference is to input, output, and files.

FORTRAN An acronym for FORmula TRANslator, a programming language designed for writing programs to solve problems that can be stated in terms of arithmetic procedures. It is the most popular of the algebraic procedure-oriented languages.

hardware The physical equipment or devices forming a computer and peripheral equipment. (See also *Software.*)

hierarchy A set of directed relations between two or more units of data such that some units of data are considered owners and others members. Each member can have one and only one owner. (See also *Network.*)

information A collection of facts or other data, especially as derived from the processing of data.

information retrieval The study of the methods and procedures for recovering specific information from stored data.

input The data to be processed.

input-output In general, the equipment used to communicate with the computer and the data involved in the communication.

interface A common boundary between automatic data processing systems or the parts of a single system.

interrupt To disrupt temporarily the normal operation of a routine by a special signal from the computer. Usually the normal operation can be resumed from that point at a later time.

key See *Label*.

label One or more characters used to identify an item of data.

language, higher-level A language such as COBOL or FORTRAN.

language, job control (JCL) The instructions required to interface the application program with the operating system.

language, procedure-oriented A machine-independent language, such as FORTRAN, that describes how the process of solving the problem is to be carried out.

language, programming A language used to prepare computer programs.

library A collection of information, usually on magnetic tapes, available to a computer.

linkage A mechanism for connecting one unit of data to another.

list, program A printed list that is the byproduct of an assembly procedure. It contains, in logical instruction sequence, all details of a program. The coded and symbolic notation is written next to the actual notations established by the assembly procedure. The program list is highly useful in the debugging of a program.

log A record of everything pertinent to a machine run: switch settings, identification of input and output tapes, copy of manual key-ins, identification of all steps, and action taken on all steps.

logic relation The relation between two units of logic data.

macro Greater in extent or size. (See also *Micro*.)

maintenance, file The periodic modification of a file to incorporate changes that occurred during a given period.

memory, primary The main internal storage.

memory, virtual A technique of automatic memory management that makes both primary and secondary storage appear as a single-level memory to the programmer.

message A group of words, variable in length, transported as a unit.

micro Smaller or more detailed. (See also *Macro.*)

mnemonic That which assists, or is intended to assist, human memory.

modem A modulator-demodulator, a device for converting one form of signal to another for equipment compatibility.

module An incremental block of storage or other building block for expanding the computer capacity.

multiplex The process of transferring data from several storage devices operating at relatively low transfer rates to one storage device operating at a high transfer rate in such a manner that the high-speed device is not obliged to wait for the low-speed devices.

multiprocessing The simultaneous execution of two or more programs or sequences of instructions by a computer.

multiprogramming The interleaved execution of two or more programs by a single computer.

network A set of directed relations between two or more units of data such that some units of data are considered owners and other members. Each member may have more than one owner. (See also *Hierarchy.*)

off-line Not in direct communication with the central processing unit of a computer.

on-line In direct communication with the central processing unit of a computer.

operation The act specified by a single computer instruction or a program step undertaken or executed by a computer. Examples are addition, multiplication, extraction, comparison, shift, and transfer.

operation, degraded The capability of a computer for operation after hardware components have failed.

operation, scheduled The periods of time during which the user plans to use specified equipment.

operator, machine The person who manipulates the computer controls, places information media into the input devices, removes the output, and performs related functions.

output The data that have been processed.

physical relationship The relation between two or more units of physical data.

pointer A link between two logical records.

printer, high-speed A printer that operates at a speed of 250 lines per minute, 100 characters per line, is considered high.

priority The sequence in which jobs will be processed by the computer as determined by the computer's priority system.

processing, batch A technique by which items are coded and collected into groups for processing.

processing, real-time The processing of information or data in a manner sufficiently rapid that the results of the processing are available in time to influence the process being monitored or controlled. Also called a real-time system.

processor An automatic data processor or arithmetic unit.

program, computer A plan or routine for solving a problem on a computer.

program, object The program that is the output of an automatic coding system. (See also *Program, Source.*)

program, source A computer program written in a language readable by humans, although it may be symbolic or algebraic. An assembler translator or compiler routine is used to transform the source program into an object program in machine language. (See also *Program, Object.*)

punch, card A machine that punches cards in designated locations to store data.

punch, paper tape A machine that punches paper tape in designated locations to store data.

queue, job A group of jobs waiting for computer processing.

reader, card A machine that senses or reads information punched into cards.

reader, magnetic tape A machine that senses or reads information recorded on a magnetic tape.

reader, paper tape A machine that senses or reads information punched into a paper tape.

recognition, magnetic ink character (MICR) A system employed by banks for automating check handling. The checks are coded with magnetic ink.

recognition, optical character (OCR) Machine identification of printed characters by means of light-sensitive devices.

record A group of related facts or fields of information treated as a unit.

record, unit A piece of punched card auxiliary equipment.

retrieval, data The recovery of specific information from stored data.

routine, diagnostic (1) A routine used to locate a malfunction in a computer or aid in locating mistakes in a computer program. (2) In general, any routine specifically designed to aid in debugging or troubleshooting.

routine, utility A standard routine used to assist in the operation of the computer. Examples are conversion, sorting, printout, and tracing routines. Same as utility program.

run The performance of one program on a computer.

set, data A circuit termination device used to provide an interface between a circuit and computer equipment.

signal The event, phenomenon, or electric quantity that conveys information from one point to another.

signal (communications) Aggregate of waves propagated along a transmission channel and intended to act on a receiving unit.

simulation A model of a working system built in the form of a computer program.

software The totality of programs and routines used to extend the capabilities of computers, and including compilers, assemblers, narrators, routines, and subroutines. (See also *Hardware.*)

storage A device into which data can be entered and from which they can be retrieved at a later time.

storage, magnetic disk A device or system consisting of magnetically coated disks on the surface of which information is stored.

storage, magnetic drum A device or system consisting of magnetically coated drums on the surface of which information is stored.

storage, magnetic strip A device or system consisting of magnetically coated strips on the surface of which information is stored.

storage, magnetic tape A device in which data are stored on magnetically coated plastic tape.

storage, primary The main internal memory of the computer.

storage, random access Information storage such that retrieval is independent of the location of the information most recently stored or retrieved.

storage, secondary Information storage that is not an integral part of the computer but is directly connected to or controlled by the computer. Examples are magnetic drums, tapes, and strips.

storage, sequential access Information storage such that items of information become available only in a one-after-another sequence as from magnetic tape storage.

structure The aggregate of units of data and their formats and relations.

switching, packet Transmission of data in groups of various sizes.

system, data management A software system that can create and update files, select, retrieve and sort data, and generate output reports.

system, operating An integrated collection of service routines for supervising the sequencing of programs by a computer. Operating systems may perform debugging, input-output, accounting, compilation, and storage assignment tasks.

teletypewriter American Telephone and Telegraph Company trade name for telegraph terminal equipment.

terminal A point in a system or communications network at which data can either enter or leave.

terminal, intelligent A terminal that can perform arithmetic and logic operations.

test, program A sample program with a known answer that is run to check machine operation.

test, system A complete simulation of the running system that is used to test the adequacy of the system.

throughput Productivity based on all facets of an operation.

time, access The interval between the instant at which data are called from a storage device and that at which delivery is completed.

time, response The interval between the instant an inquiry enters the system and that at which the response is received.

time, search The time required to locate a particular field of data in storage. Searching requires a comparison of each field with a predetermined standard until a match is obtained.

time, sharing The use of a device for two or more purposes.

total, control A sum of numbers in a specified field of a batch of records that is determined repetitiously during the processing operation so that any discrepancy from the control will indicate an error.

tube, cathode-ray An electronic tube containing a screen on which information may be stored.

unit, arithmetic The unit of a computing system that contains the circuits that perform arithmetic operations.

unit, central processing The central part of the computer system that contains the main storage, arithmetic unit, and special register groups.

unit, control The part of a computer system that contains the circuits that interpret and control the execution of instructions.

update To put into a master file changes required by current information or transactions.

Index